# SIT DOWN, *Shut Up,* and *Let Go*

## A Guide to *Losing* Control

*One mother's humorous memoir of the adventures of LIFE.*
*Making it through unthinkable loss, undeniable miracles,*
*and arriving at unimaginable wholeness.*

## JENNIFER N NAEGER

WESTBOW
PRESS
A DIVISION OF THOMAS NELSON

WestBow Press books may be ordered through booksellers or by contacting:

WestBow Press
A Division of Thomas Nelson
1663 Liberty Drive
Bloomington, IN 47403
www.westbowpress.com
1-(866) 928-1240

Because of the dynamic nature of the Internet, any web addresses or links contained in this book may have changed since publication and may no longer be valid. The views expressed in this work are solely those of the author and do not necessarily reflect the views of the publisher, and the publisher hereby disclaims any responsibility for them.

Any people depicted in stock imagery provided by Thinkstock are models, and such images are being used for illustrative purposes only.

Certain stock imagery © Thinkstock.

ISBN: 978-1-4497-4940-8 (sc)
ISBN: 978-1-4497-4939-2 (hc)
ISBN: 978-1-4497-4941-5 (e)

Library of Congress Control Number: 2012907480

Printed in the United States of America

WestBow Press rev. date: 05/22/2012

**Special thanks to:**
Kim Richardson
Stacy Limberg
Janice Burns
Tammy Fadler
Sally Borgerson

Your encouragement, kind words and contributions helped me
tremendously in this healing journey. Sometimes God believes in me
a little more than I believe in myself. Having the five of you in my corner
helped me get these words out of my heart and onto paper!

This book is dedicated to my little monkey,
**Ty Allen Naeger**
**April 29, 2001 – August 10, 2001**
Mommy loves you, buddy.


To my beloved friend,
**Mary Elizabeth Daniels**
**October 3, 1979 - August 3, 2010**
You beat me to Heaven, girl. I guess you get to sit and rock
my boy for me until I get there, someday.
I love and miss you so much!

**Special Thanks go to Amy McAllister:**
Thanks, Amy. I love you more than you will ever comprehend. I love
you in a way that I, myself, can't even comprehend. Though we haven't
seen each other for years, you have always been there, inside of my
heart. Much like Ty, you changed my life. I know that God placed you
there in that PICU at that stage in your life, so that you could be there
for me during that stage in MY life. I know that the birth of our girls
is no coincidence, and I know that there will be many more strange
similarities to uncover as we grow old and senile together; something
that some days, doesn't seem too far out of reach!

**To My Husband, Travis, and my sweet babies, Mady and Jacob:**
Without your love and God, I don't know that I would have survived.
Travis, I am so thankful that we did not turn on each other in our grief.
We have been able to grieve in different ways, but always side by side.

Mady, I know without a morsel of doubt that God placed you inside
of my weak, frail, beaten body in order to save my life. Without you, I
would have had no reason to live. The first time you looked at me with
those familiar eyes, I knew that you were a messenger.

Jacob, there has never been a doubt in my mind that you refused to be
born in order to create a beautiful memory on a horrible day. Seeing
you grow, having the honor of watching a healthy little boy doing 'boy'
things has given me a little window into what could have been with Ty.
For that, I am forever grateful.

# OH, PRECIOUS SON
## by ME

Oh, precious son . . .
Knowing all that I know now, and all that you have taught me.
I wonder what I would've done, if I'd have only seen.

Would I be the person I've become? Would I know God just as much?
Just what, exactly, would I be, had I never felt your touch?
Oh, we surrounded you with angels-on every wall, both high and low.
And Daddy's silver angel . . . praying, went all the places we could not go.

Yes, we began our ride with angels, us giving them to you . . .
And now, with wings, you dance among them—with your cousin next
to you.

Oh, it's funny how we started out, us protecting you.
My, how quickly those tables turned . . . Now that's your job- it's what you do.

But, never will I trade those days, or all the memories I hold dear.
I will preserve them in this book . . . though in my heart, you are always here.

# AUTHOR BIO

In her first published piece, author Jennifer Naeger speaks candidly and casually regarding the pain and heartbreak of losing her first child, and her unexpected relationship with God as a result.

Having given birth to a child with Down Syndrome and severe heart defects at just 24 years old, Naeger felt her life quickly spiraling out of her control. By overcoming her fears of the unknown, embracing the challenges she received, and learning to *let go* of the things she could not control, she found herself turning *to* God rather than *away* from Him.

A ten year journey of personal growth and undeniable miracles led her here, sharing her story with **you**!

Using a conversational approach to writing, readers feel as though they are talking over a cup of coffee with the author, making the message of the book somehow more approachable. Her use of light-hearted language and comedy, while telling a story so personal and painful, gives readers an opportunity to come to view her as a friend before they reach the final chapter. Throughout the pages of "Sit Down, Shut Up and Let Go," Naeger offers readers her personal recipe for a delightful, life-changing lemonade in response to the classic quote, "When life hands you lemons…"

Easy to read and delightfully 'real', Naeger's relaxed delivery of a strong Christian message uncovers an interesting conclusion:

Christians can be funny, too! Who knew?

# CONTENTS

# PREFACE:

# JOURNEY TO THE REAL ME

So, how did I get here? Why have I written this book, and perhaps more important, why do I want YOU to read it? Well, it's a long story. It has been a gradual process of becoming less myself, and more the me that God intended me to be. It's a daily investment, something that I have to consciously choose to do. But, let me just tell you, I feel more confident than I ever have in my life. Not because I am doing what I wanted to do, but because I receive affirmation that I am doing what He wanted me to do.

Throughout the chapters of this book, which is essentially my life story, you and I will meander through the innocence of a child, which we all undoubtedly took horribly for granted; only to perhaps shed a tear at the harsh reality of adulthood, something that we all can or will eventually relate to. What I hope for you, is that you will read these words, feel their presence and power, and recognize yourself someplace in MY journey.

Perhaps you are feeling alone, in the dark, and have stumbled across this book as if grasping at straws. I have been in a place so dark that there seemed to be no light. I have scoured the walls for the switch, covering every inch with my desperate fingertips; crying out in fear because the darkness crept into my soul . . . waiting for the light to come on.

I know all too well the brief feeling of peace that comes when you open your eyes, crisp pillowcase marks on your cheek; today is a new day. It lasts but a quick minute, though, before you realize that the pain and fear were not a dream. Sadly, you have awakened with the same powerless feeling, knowing that this, the thing that you are in the midst of, is larger than you, and beyond your control.

Know that I have felt these feelings. I survived, I grew, and I am here to share them with you; in an attempt to shine a light on the map that I was given. Though your path may not take the same route as mine, we are all hoping to arrive at the same destination: PEACE.

My journey to the REAL ME started when I was 24 years old. My savior came in the form of a newborn baby. He came into our world on April 29, 2001, and left just 3 ½ months later.

The time he was here, however, cannot only be measured in days, weeks or months. It should be measured in accomplishments, and by those standards, he lived _so_ long.

I had no way of knowing at the time that this tiny boy, with his blue eyes and blonde hair, would forever change me. I could never have imagined that he was sent to me as a messenger . . . that he was created to be mine, and was sent with the intention of bringing me closer to my God. You see, I had never realized that God wanted to walk by my side. I was busy living my life, loving my life, never knowing that there was MORE that God had to offer!

## Chapter 1

# TIME TO LET GO

WE HAD BEEN IN THE truck just long enough to lay the seats back and close our eyes when the cell phone rang. Travis answered, and said "Okay, we'll be right in." My heart sank and I dove up. "What?" I asked. He assured me that it was the nurse's desk, and all she said was that she needed us to come back in.

He blew it off and said he probably had gotten cranky again. We remained calm as we exited the parking garage and crossed the street, but all of a sudden I found myself running. I got a strange feeling through my body, and I could not get back to the 7th floor fast enough.

The ride in the elevator took an eternity. As the doors opened and I floated to those double doors, my heart pounded and my stomach ached as it had so many times before. The doors opened, and I saw a sea of people outside of Ty's door. The same familiar smells of sterilized bedding and antibacterial cleaners surrounded me, but this time, they faded to the background. The light above Ty's door was flashing, and a woman we did not know stopped us as we approached. "What's wrong?" I asked. "What happened, what's going on? They told us to come back . . . what's going on?"

She looked at me, and held me by both shoulders as she faced me and said "He's arrested. They're doing what they can to get him back, but he's arrested."

1

*How did I get here? Where is the rewind button? In a flash, I had gone from a carefree 24 year old to the mother of a critically ill child. Just as I had begun to feel safe and let my guard down, I got blindsided again. All I could do was keep going. I was in the game now, and there were no time-outs.*

HE'S WHAT? How can that be? Ty had been fine. He was waiting to eat and then we could go home. We only have a few hours left to wait and now you're telling me he's in cardiac arrest? Travis and I hugged and cried as that woman, a social worker, hovered around us. She made me so angry, rubbing my back and standing so close I could hear her breath. I had never met her before, and somehow she felt it appropriate to stand right there as we discussed our son. It was then that I found myself in a familiar state of helplessness. I leaned on the nurses' station desk and in front of everyone I began to pray out loud . . . just as I had done the day that Ty was born. I was pleading with God not to take him, to make him wake up and let him stay with us. I asked Travis over and over again why God would let him get this far just to take him away now. He had no answer.

It seemed like only a few minutes had passed, but it must have been more. One of Ty's other primary nurses, Jacquie, came through the double doors and looked at us confused. "What's going on?" she asked. I told her what had happened, and she assured me that she would go and help me. She entered the room full of people that we were being kept away from. As I stood there and watched the sea of people coming and going through his door, and saw that crash cart in the hall being stripped of all of its drugs, I remember saying, "This can't be right. You're not supposed to need that list by the door." Hanging by the door was always a list of meds and dosages to be given in case of a code. I had seen it a million times, but never expected it to be used.

Eventually, a doctor we knew came to talk to us. Until this point, we had been given no updates, and stood and watched outside the doors, like outsiders. All that she told us was that no one knew what happened, but he had coded. I said, "Well, did you get him back?" I fully expected her to say, "Yes, but he's not out of the woods." To my great shock, she simply shook her head no. I asked how long he had been down, and she said 45 minutes. From outside of my body somewhere, hovering between shock and calm, I rationally gave her my permission to discontinue resuscitation . . . something she did not even ask for. I don't even know where that came from, but when I told her, she said okay.

I had just given them permission to stop trying to keep my only child alive. I knew that after 45 minutes, he was gone. He had been gone for a while now, and there was no use in abusing his body any more. I let him go, and asked them to do the same.

*How had everything spiraled out of control so quickly? I had finally come to terms with the cross I was given to bear. I had accepted that my life would not be the fairy tale I had anticipated, and had fallen in love with my new "normal." What in the world was happening?*

The pregnancy was so easy. Never once did I have morning sickness. I felt wonderful, and looked forward to getting the big belly I had dreamed of for years.

Finally, in December 2000, it was time for our first ultrasound. My OB/GYN did not have ultrasound equipment in her office, so it was her practice to send her patients to St. Anthony's Mercy Medical Center in St. Louis to have a routine ultrasound. We were so ready to see the little person we had created; Travis had already made plans to be off of work so we could go together. Of course, the day of the ultrasound, we had a record amount of snowfall . . . a whole foot. I haven't quite figured this one out yet; maybe God was trying to prevent us from going, but our free will got in the way.

Determined to see this child, we put the Explorer in 4-wheel drive and went anyway. We couldn't bear the thought of having to wait to see our baby.

We got to our appointment only to find out that their physician was not able to make it in due to the weather, but we could still have the ultrasound performed by the ultrasound technician.

She showed us all of the normal things, and took a lot of pictures so that she could review them with the doctor the next day. She got pictures of everything but the heart, she said that our active child was jumping too much to get a clear picture, and asked us to come back in a week so they could try again. She said everything else seemed fine, but she knew the doctor would not be comfortable without having a good view of the heart.

Thrilled to see our baby, we were excited to think of coming back and seeing it again . . . so we agreed to come back. On the way to the truck, stomping through the snow, I asked Travis, "Do you think everything is okay? You don't think she's just pretending she couldn't see because there is something wrong, do you?" *(nudge, nudge)*.

He reassured me that everything *had* to be okay; there was no way anything could be wrong. At the time, we had 14 healthy nieces and nephews on his side of the family . . . no history of any problems on either side . . . everything was fine. We proudly took our ultrasound pictures home and enjoyed them.

We went back for our next appointment, excited to see our little bundle again. It was then that the cat was let out of the bag. The doctor came in and performed the ultrasound, and something just felt 'off.'

We were told rather quickly that our baby had some heart abnormalities. We were told that the heart forms very early. It starts as a little pod and slowly unfolds, then unfolds again, over and over again until it forms a heart with four chambers. Our baby's heart, we were told, did not finish forming. According to the doctor, it did not have the normal four chambers. The walls that form to divide the heart into four chambers were incomplete, leaving "open doors" between the chambers.

After the ultrasound, we were whisked, our bodies numb and our minds racing, into a consultation room. We sat at a table there in that stark room, where another doctor explained that our child would need at least 3 surgeries to make the heart salvageable. It was as though they possessed a little manual on this, and knew exactly what to say. The first could occur as soon as within a few days of birth. Another would follow at 3-6 months, and another at 2-4 years of age. The words echoed through my head, and I felt sick. As we sat, stunned, holding hands and crying, we struggled to understand WHY this would happen to our baby? HOW could this be? The doctors showed little emotion as they went through their script. Tearing our dreams apart with each word, they sketched examples to help explain, and I died inside as I watched the pen move across the paper.

We had prayed for this child, we had openly accepted it into our lives, even though the timing was a little off, and had never considered any other option than to be proud parents. Surely there was a mistake, and the doctors had misread the ultrasound. You hear of people being told the sex of their child, only to find out after birth that the ultrasound was misread. If they can mistake a boy for a girl, surely they can misdiagnose a heart defect, right?

## Chapter 2

# FULL-ON 'PRAYER MODE'

WELL, CUE MY FEELINGS THAT I am the bearer of all weight, all control rests in my hands, and if I don't pray right, something bad will happen. Though I had never been taught to pray, or encouraged to pray, I prayed every night. I had been a very nervous child, so I had a lot of fears for the safety of my family. You see, even though I was praying, I hadn't understood that God had everything under control. I had this fear that if I didn't pray, something bad would happen. I was such an insecure child, in a home that could be so toxic and when I prayed, I felt this compulsion to remember everything I worried about, and pray about it. Sometimes I would even have OCD type tendencies while I prayed, and repeatedly pray about the same thing. I didn't fully understand how prayer worked, but I knew, somehow, that it could. Being such a worrier, I would pray for many of the same things every night; for my parents to be safe, and to get home safely. For my little brother, who was just a toddler at the time, to be safe. I would pray that my parents would live to be very old, and the same for my brother. I felt as though if I didn't specifically pray that they would live to be really old, maybe God would let them die young. I became obsessed with not forgetting anyone in my prayers, because I felt that if I did, something bad would happen to them. Talk about pressure; In my young, unguided mind, I felt responsible for the safety and well-being of the people I loved. That is no way for a child to feel, but I was a product of my environment, and my nervous tendencies were a direct result of the uncertainty I felt in my home life.

NOW, HERE I WAS AN ADULT, SUDDENLY FEELING THE SAME INSECURITIES AND FEARS. ONCE AGAIN, I TURNED TO PRAYER.

I began to pray all the time. I remember going to one of the Sisters at our church and asking her, with all sincerity, "What do I do?" What I meant by asking this was, 'What prayer do I pray, what formula do I use, to reverse this?' I honestly thought that there must be some handy-dandy prayer in some book that she had that was going to undo this diagnosis. Apparently, I thought she had some book of Witch's Spells or something, because I just *knew* she was going to look me right in the eye and say, "Well, you just need to _____." Yeah . . . . she didn't.


I convinced myself that even if there was something wrong, God would heal our baby. Until now, I hadn't known I had so much faith. But now, I knew I had no choice! There was no way He would let something happen to the baby I prayed for. It was "all-systems-go"; we were on prayer lists all over the place. Travis's parents had sent a prayer request to a preacher they enjoyed watching on television. Watching his show one day, he made a statement that his mom was convinced was directed toward her. He stated that he had received a prayer request from a woman and the request was regarding her daughter-in-law who was having trouble during a pregnancy. He made a comment that the woman who wrote was a regular viewer and that she spent more time praying for others than she did herself, even though her health had been in danger before. Being a survivor of leukemia who often requested prayer for her loved ones, Helen just knew this was meant for her. He continued to say that he just wanted her to know that he felt the baby would be a boy, and it would be healthy. With this in mind, Helen's mind was put at ease. She took this as her sign from the Lord that everything would be okay.

We were all convinced after a while that everything would be fine, and we would have the last laugh when our healthy child entered the world. I began to believe this with every fiber of my being. It was what got me through the days and weeks that followed. Imagine the surprise on the doctors' faces when the baby is born perfect, I thought. I was convinced. I just knew it would be okay.

# Chapter 3

# THE POWER OF PRAYER

I CAN STILL REMEMBER BEING in high school and getting into the family car. My mom was taking me to school to board a bus for a weekend choir trip, and I was telling my family goodbye. My father hugged me, tears in his eyes, and said to me, "I love you. I hope nothing bad happens to me while you're gone this weekend . . . " It was this kind of mind-game that I endured most of my childhood. It was an inconspicuous form of control, a mind-game that went on over the smallest of things. Talk about guilt! It was comments like this that made me such a guilt-ridden worry-wart. I had poor posture, low self-esteem, and I carried the weight of my family's safety and well-being on my young shoulders. Sometimes I felt that since I was the only one in the family that I knew of that prayed, **I** was responsible for everyone's safety. So I prayed. A lot.

Can you remember the first time you ever realized that God had heard your prayer? I can. I was just a kid, maybe 13 or 14 years old. *I remember vividly that one night, the night God heard my prayers.* I awoke with a fear in my heart. I knew that my brother, just a toddler, and my father were going out into the woods the next morning. Something woke me from my sleep, (nudge, nudge) and this huge burden hung on my heart; a fear that something bad was going to happen. It was that feeling of impending doom, that sickness in your stomach while you wait for the other shoe to drop. I can remember that fear, that nervous feeling in my body. I prayed right then that God would protect them, wherever they went and whatever happened. I prayed and I prayed, making sure not to be vague, or to leave out any important word; because I worried that if I didn't mix that potion just right, the spell might not work.

For the first time, I received confirmation that God was indeed hearing me. Little old me, who didn't know HOW to pray, but did it anyway, making it up as I went. The next morning, when my father and brother returned home from their adventure in the woods near our home, my father told the story of how something had happened and caused the ATV they were on to overturn; but that he was able to prevent it from falling back on top of him and my brother, and they escaped uninjured.

HOLY MOLY! I knew then, that God had heard me. So, whatever it was I was doing, it must have been right! Right shoulder, left shoulder, forehead, chest . . . . backward, forward, it didn't matter. **He was hearing me. He was listening.** In a childhood where I often felt misunderstood and powerless against those around me, I was being heard by *someone*, and I felt a power I had not felt before.

### *I EXPERIENCED THE POWER OF PRAYER!*

*Now, suddenly, I was 24 years old and in more desperate need than ever. I was sure God could hear me. But would He? It was time to find out.*

*Chapter 4*

# THE ELEPHANT IN THE ROOM

IT DIDN'T TAKE LONG FOR the doctors to schedule more and more ultrasounds. It took even less time for them to begin pushing us to have an amniocentesis, which we had already refused. We tried to explain to them that even if our child did have problems, it would not change our decision to keep it. This was the child God had chosen to give to us, and nothing they could say would change our minds. It was then that they began explaining to us that these types of heart defects are often associated with Down Syndrome, and that we should really have the tests done so that we would know and be able to make educated decisions regarding our child.

We still refused. There was nothing they could say that would make us abort this baby . . . end of discussion. I later learned that approximately 90 percent of babies with Down Syndrome are aborted; 90 percent.

As time went on, we began to have more and more ultrasounds. It was as though my OB/GYN had lost all control of my case, and the perinatologists at the hospitals called all the shots. They decided when I had ultrasounds; they decided everything. I became nothing more than a number to them, just a vessel carrying a baby that they stared at on a screen. My baby became a science project.

We began to feel so helpless. Ultrasounds were in no way pleasant experiences. No longer did they show us cute little fingers and toes, they simply turned down the lights, called in other doctors, medical students, and anyone else that felt like staring at a sick baby, and just stared. They stood, with their hands on their chins, nodding their heads and saying "Uh huh, uh huh." It was not unusual for an ultrasound appointment to last for an hour or more. I laid their quietly, Travis faithfully beside me every time, and it was as though we were invisible. I understood that they needed to get as many details as they could <u>before</u> the baby was born in order to be as prepared as possible. What I didn't understand was how they could forget that we were there, forget that this was our baby, our flesh and blood, our creation. We no longer wanted to talk about what was <u>wrong</u>, we wanted to talk about what was <u>right.</u> It had 10 fingers and 10 toes, it had hair that waived beautifully in the amniotic fluid that surrounded it. It had a face, and it had a place in this world. They didn't see it that way, but we did. We refused to learn the sex of the baby. There were so many things being thrown at us already, so many of our dreams being destroyed. We wanted at least one thing to be a surprise.

Ultrasound after ultrasound, we went back for more and more punishment. We were sent to have an ultrasound and fetal echocardiogram performed by the cardiology team of St. Louis Children's Hospital in order for them to fully diagnose the baby's problems and prepare for its birth. It was at that time that we were told that the baby did, indeed, have "septal" defects (the septum is the tissue that divides the heart into four chambers, much like the septum of your nose). It also had transposition of the great vessels. In other words, the aorta and pulmonary artery were flip-flopped, which would be another big hurdle. On top of all of this was probably the most serious problem; the right ventricle was nearly non-existent. This left the baby with essentially 3 chambers, and those were not fully divided into separate chambers themselves. We were again reminded of the possibility of Down Syndrome.

I felt the words Down Syndrome radiate through my entire body every time they were uttered. I had been praying for my child's heart to be healed already, but I began finding myself praying even harder now. I am ashamed now, but I prayed that it would not have Down Syndrome. I knew that the heart could be repaired, but nothing could *fix* Down Syndrome. I was assured by everyone in our family, all of our friends, that the baby would be fine. There was just no way that it would be sick, no way it would have Down Syndrome. I prayed as hard as I could every day. I prayed, and I waited.

*Chapter 5*

# BECOMING A STATISTIC

W<small>E KEPT GOING BACK FOR</small> more ultrasounds. I wasn't quite sure why, because the cardiologists had seen what they needed to see and released us until the baby was born. We were told that there was nothing more to do but wait for it to get here. The perinatologists at the other hospital were not so agreeable. They seemed to think I needed to come in at least once a month for an ultrasound. I began to think it was just to charge my insurance company $700 dollars for each visit, but was afraid to refuse the ultrasounds. I did not want to jeopardize my baby's health, even though I knew that the cardiologists had already seen all they needed to see. What else are these doctors looking for, I asked myself? WHYYYYYYYYY ARE THEY DOING THIS? With each ultrasound came a new warning. For a while, I was told I had an abundance of amniotic fluid, which could be dangerous. So every two weeks I went in for an ultrasound to check the levels of amniotic fluid. I was told that with too much fluid, my uterus could be fooled into thinking I was further along than I was, and could go into premature labor. They said my baby could not live if it was born prematurely, not with the heart problems it already had. So, even though my OB/GYN never felt as though the measurements she took seemed unusual, I still went back time and time again for more ultrasounds. I did that about four times before they decided that the levels of fluid were not dangerous to the baby and were not high enough to possibly cause premature labor.

*At this point, I really should have just spoken up, and found my voice. I should have told them that ENOUGH WAS ENOUGH! But, I didn't. I was scared. And when we are scared, we sometimes ignore our inner voice. We ignore our gut feelings, and we go into 'emergency mode.' I was there . . . . I had become a robot. Not God's robot, but the Doctors' robot.*

Next came another scare with the possibility of another problem with the baby. Of course, as luck would have it, this was the only ultrasound Travis could not go to. Here I was again, a big ole beached whale, lying on a table, cold goo squirted all over my belly . . . like a fish in a tank, being stared at. They stared, they watched, they pointed, they mumbled . . . .

There, all alone, I was told by a very insensitive doctor that she felt my baby looked to have duodenal atresia. The duodenum is a part of the intestine, and she explained to me that she saw signs of a narrowing or possible total closing off of the intestines at the duodenum. This, she explained, could be the cause of the additional amniotic fluid. She said that a normal fetus swallows and digests a certain amount of fluid. If our baby had this duodenal atresia, it would not be able to completely pass the fluid through the intestine. Thus, if no fluid is being digested, it is staying in the sac around the baby, resulting in an abundance of fluid. She went on to explain that if this was the case, our baby would require yet another surgery to repair the atresia. How extensive the surgery would be could not be determined until after birth, at which time they would find out if there was only a narrowing or if it was totally closed off.

Well, why don't you just kick the pregnant girl in the teeth while she's down on the ground? Anything else??? I mean, really. Here I was, no husband with me, no one to drive me home . . . This kid wasn't getting here today or tomorrow, could you not have delayed the dropping of this bomb for one more visit? Knowing what I know now, sometimes I would love to go back and have a 'talk' with this woman . . . but that wouldn't be very Christ-like of me, would it? (Damn Free-Will!!!)

We had several more ultrasounds, with different doctors every time, to evaluate the baby's abdomen. We were finally told that no other doctors could see signs of duodenal atresia; they were unsure of what the first doctor had seen. Of course, by now, the insurance company had been charged a few thousand more dollars for unnecessary ultrasounds.

$$$ CHAAAAAA-CHIIIIIING! $$$

*Again, still no backbone grown yet on my part. Still numb, floating around in an enormous body, scared to death and becoming more of a robot every day, I just kept going back. It's kind of like how no one tells you that once you have kids, you will probably pee when you jump. Yeah, no one ever sits you down and tells you that you are in control of your body---and you don't HAVE to do everything the doctor tells you to do.*

*Geez, why didn't someone tell me this??*

## Chapter 6

# CAN YOU HEAR ME <u>NOW</u>??

IT DIDN'T TAKE LONG FOR them to find something else to scare us with. In January or February, we were told that our baby's femur length had begun to "fall off of the charts." They had ranges which they felt were "normal," and our baby's femur (thigh bone) growth had slowed down. This was a red flag to them, and they became concerned, once again, that this was another indication of possible Down Syndrome.

*Obviously, the nudging is not working.*
*Time for Plan B:*
*(Ummmm . . . . tap, tap, tap: "IS THIS THING ON???? Yeah, this is God. Pay attention to this part, okay? CAN YOU HEAR ME NOW???)*

Again, my heart sank. They had pounced all over every bit of excitement I felt every time I went in for an ultrasound.

*It was like going out onto the playground, picking out the weakest, frailest kid, and just knocking him down and beating him to a bloody pulp. Showing no mercy, holding no punches, just taking every ounce of 'self' that he has and just ripping it to shreds.*

17

In fact, it had gotten to the point where we would go in for an ultrasound, which lasted approximately one hour, and often did not even get any pictures of our baby. They didn't even try to humor us now . . . they were all business.

Don't get me wrong, my hat goes off to any physician who chooses such an occupation. Only God could create such a human, who can deal with such heartbreaking matters of life and death on a daily basis. But, seriously, some of these people need to take a step back and re-evaluate their approach. When you become so distant from your patient that you can no longer nurture the soul of the person you are poking at, you need to make a change.

I went back to my OB/GYN and discussed the femur length with her. She also explained to me that short legs were sometimes an indication of Down Syndrome. (So help me, God, this was getting ridiculous! I still didn't catch on! 'Blatantly obvious, party of one. Your table is now available!')

Our next ultrasound was performed by yet another doctor. This woman, however, was very nice. A very tall, thin yet wide woman herself who actually had a fairly odd physical shape, she explained to us that the femur length could mean nothing more than that our baby had short legs. She even used the example that, had there been ultrasounds when she was being born, the doctors would surely have worried that something was wrong with her because her legs are so long and seemingly out of proportion with the rest of her body.

This came as a relief to both Travis and me. Although the two of us are nearly the same height, my legs are some 2-3 inches longer than his. We decided that our baby was just going to be long-waisted like Travis, and we no longer worried. Yep! That has GOT to be all it is!

Of course, the doctors were still worried. I was then brought in continuously for rigorous ultrasounds to monitor the baby's femur length. We were told that if it continued to decline, further measures may be necessary. Perhaps the baby was not getting the proper nutrients to grow and develop normally, or perhaps it had Down Syndrome.

I worried more and more about those two words, Down Syndrome. What if our baby did have Downs? What would we do? I began to get more and more signs which, I know now, were sent to prepare me for what would be very obvious at birth.

## Chapter 7

# BUCKLE UP, CAPTAIN OBVIOUS.
# IT'S ABOUT TO GET BUMPY!

I WAS WORKING AT JOACHIM-PLATTIN Ambulance District as the office manager during my pregnancy, a job I had had since I was 18 years old. I didn't just have friends there, I had family. The only full-time female to be found there, I had "brothers" galore that understood all this medical jargon and explained it to me as best they could. To this day, they all hold such a special place in my heart, and I love them all.

I am so thankful that I had worked there long enough to understand medical terminology, to have some understanding of how things worked. I was fairly well-versed in the medical world; I could at least hold my own in a conversation, as long as it did not get too technical. Travis was not as lucky. He struggled with the things that were thrown at us, and felt rather helpless at times.

It was at work, actually, that I first started "being prepared" by God for what lay ahead. As you probably know, Down Syndrome is not exactly common. It's not as though you run across people with Down Syndrome every day, or even every week. However, in one day, I was given two different ambulance reports for two different children who were picked up by our paramedics who both had Down Syndrome. What were the odds,

I thought? I'd worked there for six years and had maybe only seen 2 or 3 reports for patients with Downs; how strange that two would be picked up in the very same day. Though I wanted to blow it off to coincidence, (there's that word again!) I knew in my heart that this was significant information.

Within a week, I received the latest issue of the baby magazine I had subscribed to. Who should appear on the cover but a beautiful little girl with Down Syndrome.

*I continued to get little clues like this for weeks, and stored them all in the back of my mind. I knew in my heart that our baby would have Downs. I knew that the doctors were trying to tell me, without <u>telling</u> me. I knew, but I didn't want to know.*

Travis didn't want to talk about it. It was impossible, he thought. There was no way, and I was just being paranoid. He used the example of "You probably never noticed blue Ford Explorers with grey trim before we got one, did you? Now you notice every one that passes." He felt I was doing the same thing with Downs kids. I was *looking* for them, so I was noticing them. Maybe he was right, I thought. I may have *thought* it, but I didn't really *believe* he was right.

My mom would always ask me, "So what if it does have Down Syndrome, what difference does it make? Will it change the way you love your baby?" Of course not, and I knew that, but I still worried. What would it look like? Would it still look like us, or would it look like every other child with Downs? I didn't know the first thing about Down Syndrome, and that scared me. But, I wasn't about to get information on it, though. That would mean that I had accepted the fact that it may be true. To accept that it may be true may give God the impression that I *wanted* it to be true. I certainly did not want that. I'm not proud of the way I felt, but it's true.

What made it worse was that no one else could understand. Our family cared, of course. But, at the end of the day, they could go to bed and wake up without their futures hanging in the balance. We did not have this luxury, though. The weight of the cross we were carrying was becoming more than we could bear. Despite all the positive thinking in the world, we were being dragged to our knees.

# Chapter 8

# NESTING AND PLANTING . . .
# NESTING AND PLANTING

WE CONTINUED TO LOOK FORWARD to the birth of our child, and had 3 different showers. It was during these brief moments of celebration that we could temporarily escape from all of our fear and actually feel excited for our baby's arrival. We allowed ourselves to get carried away, like children at a parade. For a few hours, we were a 'normal' couple, expecting a 'normal' baby.

Travis put together all of the fun things we got, and we played with all the vibrating bouncy seats and toys we could get our hands on. I had always wanted a round crib that I had seen years before in a store, and we began looking for it. Of course, by this time, it was nowhere to be found. Finally, a clerk at one of the stores remembered the crib and gave me the name and website of the manufacturer.

The cribs ranged in price from $800-$4000, which was way out of my price range. Lucky for us, Travis's uncle, Eddie, was thrilled to MAKE the bed for us himself. This was so exciting for me, having something to look forward to for once, and I was so thrilled to finally see it in person. The bed was beautiful; even more beautiful than the $4,000 bed in Hollywood. What a relief, I thought, something finally went right.

We finished the nursery with time to spare. I had originally planned to do it in Tigger and Pooh, but after the baby's diagnosis, I decided angels were more appropriate. This baby would need all the angels it could get. We found a beautiful picture done by Anne Geddes of a newborn baby lying safely in the arms of a huge concrete angel statue.

The picture moved me. I decided I had to have it, and that would be the theme for the room. I found there were many more Anne Geddes prints with everything from babies with angel wings to men with angel wings holding babies. They were so beautiful, and I knew they were just what I needed.

The room went from a nursery to an art gallery. The walls were denim blue. I wanted a shelf to go around the entire room approximately a foot from the ceiling, and Travis set to work. He worked for hours and hours constructing shelving that did just that. We painted the shelves a bright yellow, and the walls above the shelves were painted eggplant. The ceiling was done to resemble a sky, with a giant sun and clouds. By the time I was done hanging my angel prints, the place was full, there was no blank wall to be found. The baby got its first Christmas gift from Daddy before it was even born . . . a beautiful silver angel that sat about 8 inches tall. The angel knelt with its hands folded neatly in its lap, its head looking down. It was perfect to place on top of the tall armoire, as though looking down into the crib.

We collected so many stuffed animals and toys that the shelves quickly filled up. We couldn't resist hitting every sale on baby clothes until the closet and the armoire filled up, too. We just knew our baby was a boy, though it had never been confirmed. We bought a few yellow things, but for the most part everything was blue. Travis wanted no part of anything pink or frilly; he knew he would have a son. In the event that it was a girl, he said, she would just have to wear blue. So that was that; we bought more clothes than we knew what to do with. This was our release, this was how we got ourselves excited again after the doctors would break our hearts.

In fact, Travis couldn't resist, he had to go to the grocery store and buy some Dreft detergent so I could wash the clothes. I can still picture us standing in front of the dryer, pulling open the door and sniffing every last bit of scent out of that first batch of fluffy, snuggly baby clothes. They smelled so good, and it was so hard to wait to put someone inside of them.

Travis eventually got to the point of being uncontrollably sick of me still being pregnant. He wanted this baby to get here so bad he could taste it. I, on the other hand, was a little more content being pregnant. I knew that our baby was safe and healthy as long as it was still inside of me. I feared the unknown of what would happen when it emerged, and wanted to keep it safe as long as I could. I laughed so hard when Travis told me I was being *shiesty*, I needed to stop hogging all the fun with the baby and let it be born already so *he* could play, too. He was ready, and I was petrified.

We were closing in on my due date of May 5, 2001, Cinco de Mayo. Travis had decided that I did not need to be working forty hours a week anymore, and starting two weeks before my due date, I began taking each Thursday and Friday off. That second Thursday and Friday, I convinced Travis to take off work with me so that we could have some time together. We had recently put in a large garden pond, along with a porch swing I had longed for. We spent our days off swinging on the porch swing and doing things we never did, like going out for breakfast. It was wonderful. Doing construction, he often worked long hours, and we hadn't had much alone time.

During those days together, I had a serious case of what I found out later was nesting. I worked all day in the yard, planting more flowers than I knew what to do with. Travis laughed at me as I wallowed around in the yard like a beached whale trying to plant these flowers. Somehow, during this pregnancy, I gained 60 pounds. By this time, I was huge and not very agile. That didn't keep me from working for hours in my gardens. I planted and planted until I had blisters on my hands . . . then I planted some more.

On Friday, Travis got the bright idea to give me his rolling stool from the garage. That made it even easier for me to roll my now large self all over the yard planting even more. Imagine for a minute what my neighbors must have thought! Travis's mom stopped by that afternoon to find me just returning from the nursery, where I bought even more flowers. She couldn't help but laugh at me sitting on that stool, my legs apart with my giant belly hanging between them, struggling to reach the ground to plant my new purchases. I'm sure the neighbors thought I'd lost my mind, but I didn't care, I was on a roll.

## Chapter 9

# BARBECUE AND BABIES

SATURDAY WE DECIDED TO BARBECUE and invite a few friends over. We cleaned and cooked all day and had a great time enjoying the beautiful late-April weather. My friend, Mary, was among the friends that were with us that day. She laughed and teased me that I would probably go into labor while they were visiting . . . and she was right. Around 5 p.m. that evening, while enjoying barbecue that seemed unusually delicious to me, I had my first contraction.

I immediately called Travis's mom. Having done this ten times, I considered her an expert on early labor, and wondered if this was "it." She told me to keep writing down how far apart the pains were and let her know if they got closer or more consistent.

I then called my mom to give her the huge news. I didn't want to call her and get her excited without talking to my mother-in-law first, just in case I was jumping the gun. I told her I would call her back if anything changed, and got off of the phone. I continued to eat my dinner and wonder, "Is this it?"

Sure enough, by about 10 pm I decided this was, in fact, "it." I tried to lie down to sleep, but the pains got worse. I remember finding myself hanging from our chest of drawers, knees bent, caught in the midst of a contraction that felt as though I may actually turn inside-out right there!

No wonder my mother-in-law always told me, "Don't worry. You'll know!" Oh, I knew alright!

By about 11:30 pm, I could wait no longer. They were about 4-5 minutes apart and really starting to hurt. Off to the truck we went.

We had already decided to deliver the baby at Barnes Hospital in St. Louis, some hour and twenty minutes away. This hospital was next door to St. Louis Children's Hospital, and the two were connected by passage ways. If something was wrong with the baby, it would be sent to Children's, so it only made sense to deliver at Barnes so that I was close by. I was still convinced that nothing would be wrong, and we would go home in a day or two with our beautiful baby.

SURELY I HAD PRAYED ENOUGH. SURELY I HAD COMBINED JUST THE RIGHT WORDS, SPOKEN TO JUST THE RIGHT PEOPLE, AND PRAYED THE PROPER NUMBER OF TIMES TO UNDO ANYTHING THAT HAD BEEN SEEN PREVIOUSLY BY THE DOCTORS. I KNEW PRAYER WORKED. IF EVER THERE WAS A TIME FOR MY LUCK TO KICK IN, IT WAS <u>NOW</u>!

*Chapter 10*

# DENIAL, THY NAME IS JENNIFER

LABOR IS PRETTY EASY, I thought. The ride to the hospital was a little sketchy, though. Travis was nervous, and I was in pain. This combination resulted in what could only be described as a reenactment of a high-speed chase! I was attempting to play it cool. I pulled and tugged on the passenger-side door handle during contractions, trying to downplay my fear and pain. Meanwhile, Travis's mom was in the backseat scared for her life! That poor woman had no idea what she was signing up for when she agreed to let us pick her up on our way to the hospital!

I arrived at the hospital dilated to 2 or 2 ½ cm, and received my epidural by 3cm. Once I got the epidural, I was high as a kite. We had been up all night, but I was wide awake. I couldn't understand why Travis and our moms were so tired. I had no pain, and was ready to rock and roll.

My labor went on until about 10:30 am, when they decided it was time to start pushing. Still convinced that everything would be okay, and somewhat under the influence of the narcotics in my epidural, all the fear had left me.

We were taken to the operating room to deliver because there would be more room there for all of the pediatricians and cardiologists that would be standing by during the delivery. Travis and I thought it was silly to have them all there, since nothing was going to be wrong, but we agreed and got wheeled down the hall. Travis suited up in his lovely yellow gown, which he put on backward. He even got the little paper shoe covers and hat, which my friend Chrissy caught on film.

Once in the operating room, the mood changed a little. Under the glare of the bright lights and cold stark reality of stainless steel surroundings, I started to feel a little nervous. With about 20 specialists staring at me, I was instructed to push when I felt the next contraction; but that was going to be a little difficult since I couldn't actually *feel* the contractions. "Sure," I agreed, "no problem. You just tell me when I'm supposed to be feeling them and I'll try to push." Of course, I couldn't feel whether or not I was pushing, but I thought I was. The nurses and doctors agreed that I was pushing very well, although I couldn't tell what in the world I was doing. One of the doctors rolled a mirror over for me to look in, so that I could see what I was doing since I couldn't feel anything. I watched as that little head emerged, though I couldn't see the face. Travis watched in awe as our child emerged for the first time.

This was it, I thought. Our moment of glory, the moment we have been waiting for. They will all be shocked when they see how perfect he is, how healthy his heart is.

In about 2 seconds, the fun was over. The baby was whisked away to the corner of the room without anyone even telling us if it was a boy or a girl. "What is it?" I screamed, and waited for a response. Someone finally said "It's a boy!" Travis and I hugged and kissed. We knew all along it would be a boy, and we were right. Maybe the preacher's message on television *was* meant for us. Maybe we were right about him being healed, too.

It didn't take long for me to begin to wonder about his heart, though. Off in the corner, I saw nothing but heads and white coats surrounding our son. Something was going terribly wrong, because this was NOT what I had counted on! One of the doctors came over to get Travis, and brought him to see our son, Ty Allen. He came back and told me he was beautiful and everything was fine, but I knew better. I still hadn't seen him, but I knew something was not right. Next, I saw something that still sends chills down my spine. Without being able to see Ty, I could see the doctors pull out a laryngoscope and begin intubating him. I knew what was happening from working with Paramedics for years, I had seen it before. Travis, on the other hand, had no idea what was going on. Without even thinking, I began to say "Oh my God, they're tubing him . . . they're tubing him. Something's wrong." Travis again assured me that everything was fine, but I didn't agree. Without hesitation, I did something I had never done before. I began to pray out loud. My prayers had been something I had always kept to myself, praying while I was alone. Suddenly I was begging God to let our son be okay and to take care of him. I was begging right in front of everyone in the room, and I didn't care. I knew I had to ask God for help. He was the only one who could control the situation, and I wasn't ashamed to beg.

A few minutes later, a doctor emerged from the crowd of coats and came to my bedside. Still being sewn up, I sat helplessly as she said the words I didn't want to hear. "We're getting him stabilized, and once he gets to Children's, we'll have to run some tests. *He does have some signs . . .*"

Without her even finishing her sentence, I knew what she meant. Signs of Downs is what she meant. I immediately began to question Travis, since he had been allowed to see Ty. He kept telling me that he looked normal to him, just a beautiful baby boy. He said she didn't know what she was talking about, and that that's not what she meant.

**He's sweet, but he's a horrible liar.**

31

## Chapter 11

# I WANT A DO-OVER!

AFTER WHAT SEEMED LIKE AN eternity, a break began to form in the sea of white coats that surrounded the baby that so far, to me, had no face.

As the sea parted, an incubator emerged. In it was my son. As they approached my bedside, I could see him for the first time. It was obvious, he did have Downs. While I would love to say that he was the most beautiful thing I had ever seen, he wasn't. I don't mean because he had Downs, I mean because his color was terrible. He had a tube hanging out of his mouth and he was being bagged. His face was red, his eyes were swollen, and he just did not look healthy. My hopes of his being healed were shattered, he was indeed sick. I got to touch him through a hole in the side of the incubator for only a few seconds. I remember distinctly looking at my swollen hand through that hole, my fingers donning acrylic nails with a French manicure. It was the beginning of a new life for me, a life that would no longer accommodate things like manicures. I would soon lose myself for quite some time. I would no longer recognize the girl in the mirror, her roots showing, her hair not fixed, wearing no makeup. It was all on the brink in that moment, as I poked my hand through that hole. The beginning of the end of the old me . . . I just didn't know it. With that brief touch accounted for, they took him away. They told us that he would be taken directly to Children's Hospital for an echocardiogram and we should be able to come over and check on him in about an hour.

I cried uncontrollably, and Travis tried to console me. He was so strong, and I was a mess. <u>This was not the way things were supposed to happen.</u> He was supposed to be born, and they would shout "It's a boy, a beautiful boy!" Then they would wipe him off, wrap him up and lay him on my chest. We would look lovingly into his eyes, and we would be a family. Instead, Travis did not get to cut the cord, we did not get to hold him, and we only saw him through glass, like a human spectacle. It was a flashback to all those months spent lying on that table, Doctors staring at a screen . . . Once again, my boy was an "it."

I was pushed back to my room, while Travis went to talk to our family and friends. I remember crying to our moms and friends as I said over and over, "He has Downs, and they tubed him. He does have Downs. I knew it, he has Downs." They tried to console me, but it was as though it was a dream. I've never felt so strange and out of place in my life; everything was in slow motion. My life was changing forever, and I wasn't sure how to handle it. No one could fix it for me, no one even knew how to try.

Soon after, the nurse asked me if I could stand. I had just given birth moments before, but she said that the sooner I stood and got in the shower, the sooner I could go to see my baby. With that, I stood and walked to the restroom. She started the shower for me and stood outside while I showered in a daze. When I came out, she fitted me with a gown. Travis came back, and I put on my robe. Within just a few minutes of having a baby, I was clean and in a wheelchair being pushed through passageways to St. Louis Children's Hospital NICU, a place I was convinced I would never see again after our tour months before.

As we approached the big double doors that read N.I.C.U., I felt as though I could throw up. Even thinking about it now puts knots in my stomach. Travis pushed me up to the window where the secretary sat, and we asked for our son, by name, for the first time. We were told that he had not returned from his tests yet, and we could wait across the hall.

By this time, more family had arrived, I think. We filled the room and waited. I can only remember bits and pieces of this waiting, and can only picture some of the faces that sat around that big table with us as we sat for over an hour. It is as though I am trying to remember details of a nightmare; everything is hazy. Much like a movie, in which someone is remembering events, the memories come in flashes; like blocks of time. It is difficult to piece together, yet as I do, my stomach still churns to this day.

Finally, a doctor came in to talk to us. I honestly cannot remember if he talked to us very much or just took us back to see Ty. We went through those big double doors, and straight into a world of beds full of tiny babies, beeping monitors and chaos. As we approached our son, I felt so sick. I stood from my wheelchair and looked at him. I am so sad to say that he didn't even feel like he was mine. It was as though I was visiting someone else's child. I don't know why, but that's how I felt.

*Chapter 12*

# WILL HE EVER OPEN HIS EYES?

T HAT FIRST DAY WAS A blur. I remember seeing Ty for a while, and then taking the long journey back to the other hospital to our room. While there with some of our family, a cardiologist came in to dicuss Ty's condition.

"It's just as we expected it to be." He said. 'Hold the damn phone,' I thought. 'It's sure as hell not how I thought it was going to be!'

He went on to tell us everything we had been told after that first ultrasound. They would be giving Ty medication through an IV to keep a part of his heart open that normally shuts shortly after birth. By keeping this open, they would be keeping him stable until they could decide when to do the first surgery. It could be tomorrow, it could be a week from now, the doctor explained. We will just have to wait and see.

My worst nightmare was coming true, and there was nothing any of us could do but wait?

That night, I felt so hollow, so empty. For months I had felt that little person moving inside of me, and I knew that he was safe. I took comfort in knowing that I had him nestled safely inside of me, and I felt in control. Now, my once full belly just seemed to hang there like jello, and I felt no more movement. As I laid down to try to sleep, I asked Travis to move his bed next to mine. "Hold me," I said, "Hold me as tight as you can and don't let go." He couldn't seem to hold me tight enough. I felt so alone, empty and afraid. If he had let go for even a second, I think I would have gone insane. I had never felt so needy before. I just wanted to rewind 24 hours and pretend the day had never happened, but I couldn't.

The next morning, I awoke still snuggled as close to Travis as I could get. Part of me wanted to rush over to see Ty, and part of me wanted to stay right where I was. It was as though we were all alone in that hospital. No one came in to check on us; we slept all night with no interruptions. I guess they knew what we had been through and left us alone, but I thought someone would be coming in to check on me. A nurse finally came in, pressed on my belly, checked my stitches and said everything was okay. We took showers and got ready to head over to see Ty. It was like our own hotel room; no one came in but a maintenance man to check on something.

As we wheeled past the nurses' station, we had to do no more than tell them where we were going. They simply nodded, and we went on our way.

At this point, I don't think we even knew any of the details, such as weight, length, exact time of birth. There had been a birth, there had been a baby whisked off, and there had been tears. Those were the only things I was certain of. It was as though we were in a twilight zone.

We had to ask a nurse at the NICU for that information, and it took her a while to get it and write it down for us.

7 pounds 1 ½ ounces

20 inches

11:04 am

In this alter universe, Ty was not a person. He had no name, he was just baby boy Naeger. No newborn photos were taken, and no staff shouted 'Congratulations!!!'

He just laid there, never opening his eyes, with more monitors and IV's than I had ever seen. For a while he was on oxygen by nasal canula, which they taped to his face. He had an allergic reaction to the tape, and looked horrible. He had big, raised red marks across his face, and looked like he had been abused. The poor thing wasn't even being fed, he just had an IV. I had planned on breastfeeding, but that was quickly pushed to the back of my mind.

We finally got to hold him, but only briefly. They didn't want him to be overly stimulated. Even when he was being held, he didn't open his eyes. The nurse reassured me that that was okay, but it scared me.

Family visited off and on that day, and commented on how cute he was, found features that resembled other family members, and they all said that he didn't look like he had Downs to them. I know they were only trying to console me, and I love them for it. I knew by the extra skin on his neck, the shape of his eyes, and just my maternal instinct that he had Down Syndrome, even if they tried to disagree.

Even as I held him that day, I still felt no bond. I worried and felt guilty about it, but could not deny it. I began to think that maybe he was not going to live, and that is why I subconsciously was not letting myself get attached. In the back of my mind, I wondered if he would make it.

For two days he didn't open his eyes even once. He did respond to our voices, though. When we would talk to him and stroke his soft skin, his oxygen saturation would go up. A normal, healthy person will "sat" at 100%. Because of his condition, Ty's sats bounced between 82 and 89%. We were told that the doctors would prefer they be more in the seventies, because the higher the percentage, the more oxygen was being diverted to the lungs and taken from the rest of the body. When we would talk to him, his sats would shoot up to as high as 97%. This was not desirable according to doctors, but it let us know our son heard us, even if he wouldn't open his eyes.

## Chapter 13

# THE PHONE CALL

WE WERE STILL WAITING FOR the doctors to decide when to do the first surgery. They were waiting for Ty's oxygen saturations to level out, which could take a few days. Once that happened, they would know that he was ready for surgery.

Much to our surprise, the phone in our room rang that second night, when Ty was just over a day old. The voice on the other end was the same cardiologist who had visited our room the day before. He wanted to let us know that they 'saw no reason to wait'; they would be performing Ty's surgery the next morning. I know now that that must have really meant, "This kid can't wait. He's gonna die if we don't operate." But, being numb, I didn't delve into it any further.

My heart sank again. I had not yet even adjusted to the chaos going on around us and they were ready to do surgery? I was still in denial that my baby wasn't even in the room with me. I was supposed to be glowing! The room was meant to be filled with balloons and flowers, and visitors were supposed to fight over who would hold this beautiful baby next.

Instead, I was in a stark room. There was no buzz of excitement, or at least not the good kind. I felt so overwhelmed, yet part of me just wanted to get it over with. I hung up the phone and told Travis what the doctor had said. We immediately got on the telephone to let our family know that in just a few hours, Ty would have his first open-heart surgery. It was the phone call I never thought I would have to make.

## Chapter 14

# WHAT DO YOU MEAN,
# IT'S NOT ENOUGH?

IT WAS MAY 1, 2001. We made sure we got over to Children's early and stopped by the chapel. The chapel wasn't exactly what I had hoped for; it was just a room with some chairs along the wall and a small altar. On the altar, however, was a board where you could hang prayer requests. I struggled to hold the pen in my hand, and I shakily wrote down "Please pray for our 2-day old son having open-heart surgery today."

This tiny scrap of paper served as a tangible sign of what I, until now, had not fully wrapped my mind around. It was then that it truly hit me; he was only 2 days old, and they would be cutting his little chest open.

We left the chapel rather emotionally, and continued upstairs to be with Ty before surgery. We walked with him as far as we could, and kissed his tiny face over the side of his tall bed. He was just a speck on that adult-size gurney, and this task was beginning to feel insurmountable; this cross, too much to bear.

It was then that I became more emotional, after it was explained to me that he would probably need blood transfusions. It was another blow to my weak, frail soul, thinking of him losing blood from his tiny little body. We were never told this before, or we would have given blood for him. WHY had we not been told? The thought of him getting someone else's blood disturbed me terribly, but it was too late now. We were told that we could donate for next time, because there would be more surgeries to follow.

Ahhh, yes. More surgeries . . . . I hadn't even begun to wrap my mind around this one, and there it was again; the impending doom of knowing that THIS was not our only hurdle to jump. There would be more. The race was far from over; we were only warming up on the sidelines.

We waited with our families for what seemed to be an eternity. Most of that time is very hazy to me. I just know that I had a strange, detached feeling. What in the hell was wrong with me? Why did I feel like I was floating above this situation, not living within it? I couldn't control my feelings, and it bothered me. Heck, it flat out pissed me off! I felt like I had no control of any part of this situation. I could not control my feelings toward Ty, and though I longed to bond with him and love him more than life itself; I felt a disconnect between us. I could not control his physical health, I could not stop his need for this surgery . . . I couldn't control anything! All of my prayer had not been enough. My dedication, my devotion to God had not saved him!

I still didn't feel as close to him as I thought I should, and I feared in the back of my mind that that was God's way of preparing me for death. I was really wondering if he would make it through surgery, and that maybe it was best if I wasn't attached to him yet.

After hours that seemed more like days, doctors came and told us that everything had gone fine. They had put a shunt in Ty's heart to help with the blood flow, and he would need some time to recover.

He was moved to the Pediatric Intensive Care Unit, or PICU. Not only were there post-op babies in this unit, but very ill children as well. This was a much different atmosphere than the NICU. The NICU was just a giant room filled with fear. Cribs filled the room, which I can only describe as being in 'compartments', yet we were all open to one another. One nurse would have several tiny patients, and the sounds of other baby's monitors and other parents' weeping felt like imminent doom.

Here in the PICU, the doom was still palpable. However, this unit was divided into individual rooms. With the front wall of each room being comprised of glass, we were again a spectacle. Each room had a nurse's desk just outside the door, and each nurse had just one patient. This PICU would prove to be both my worst nightmare *and* my favorite place, in the weeks to follow.

We were given a wonderful nurse named Ron. He was a tall, handsome guy, probably late 20's . . . not exactly what you expected to see when you thought "male nurse." He was not overly friendly, he did not hold our hands, he did not sugar coat things. What he did was better. He explained everything that he did to us. He explained the monitor over the bed to us, which displayed Ty's blood pressure, oxygen saturation, heart rate, etc. He knew that we were unfamiliar with the machines, gadgets and noises going on around us. I'm sure he could see the distress on our 24 year old faces as we seemed to age years over the course of minutes and hours, and I'm sure it wasn't the first time he had seen it. One of the first suggestions he gave us, which we kept with us through the lengthy hospitalization, was don't be a "monitor watcher." He explained to us that, like anything else, the monitor could make false displays depending on whether a lead had come off of Ty's chest, or whether his pulse oximeter came off of his finger or toe. When these things would occur, the monitor would sound in order to alert the nurse. So, just because the monitor sounded didn't mean that something was wrong with our son.

As I watched Ron work with Ty, his head nearly touching the warming lights that hovered above the bed, I saw a diligent, thorough nurse. He sweated profusely as he worked, frequently wiping sweat from his forehead. I knew some of this could be attributed to the lights beating down on him, but some of it was from pressure.

He took his work very seriously, which I admired. For the first time, Travis and I felt some kind of peace; comforted by his up-front attitude and "realness." He wasn't the sweet old lady there to comfort us; he was there to do everything in his power to keep our son healthy. We quickly made mental note of Ron, and he was later put on Ty's Primary Care Nurse list, which assured that if Ron was working and was available, he would be Ty's nurse for that shift. When you live your life as up in the air as we were, you learn to take comfort in the little things. One of those, we learned, is knowing *who* is caring for your child. Knowing Ty was in the hands of one of his primary nurses was like the silver lining on the clouds of despair.

It was only a few hours after surgery, but we noticed that there still seemed to be a lot of commotion in Ty's room. Soon we were told by a cardiologist that the shunt they had put in did not seem to be large enough. It was an unlikely situation, one they did not often see, but it was true. I remember standing there in the hall, looking at this surgeon, whom to this day I refer to as Super Man, because he resembled Christopher Reeves. I wanted to climb on top of him and choke the life right out of him! I distinctly remember asking him, "What do you MEAN, it's not enough? How can it not be enough? You never said this could happen!" They would need to open his chest again and evaluate the situation. I immediately asked what the risk was for performing yet another surgery, and was told just what I feared . . . there was a definite increased risk of complications, but they had no choice. Ty could not survive unless they did something.

Our tiny son was once again taken to the operating room, just hours after he had left. After a shorter surgery time, the doctors explained that they had left the first shunt in, and put in a second as well.

I would learn years later that this surgery earned Ty a nickname among the PICU staff; Two-Shunt Ty.

In this new world, there was little that resembled anything we were accustomed to. I found myself feeling alone though I was surrounded by people. The one thing that provided an escape was food. Inside of the hospital cafeteria area were several fast-food restaurant stations. Travis would push me in a wheelchair down to the cafeteria. Though I was clad in a hospital gown and plaid robe, undoubtedly looking like a train wreck,I would find myself suddenly relieved. For these short thirty minutes or so, I could pretend I was someplace else. I found myself looking forward to mealtime, because it was my one chance at feeling normal. To this day, I can remember the feeling of relief that came with being in that place. I longed to eat again. Not because I was physically hungry, but because I was emotionally starving. It was this experience that made me able to identify with food addicts who describe the feeling of euphoria that accompanies self-medicating with food. I understand now what they feel, regardless of what drove them to *need* to feel it.

## Chapter 15

# THANK YOU, GOD, FOR NURSES!

WE WERE RELIEVED IN A way, and scared to death in another of what lie ahead. We didn't know the first thing about what was happening, what *would* happen, or what *could* happen.

Initially, we were told by the cardiologists that average recovery/hospitalization time was 7-10 days. For a few days, we thought we would be home in that amount of time. We were still in our initial phases of this obstacle, and had not yet learned the ropes. We hung on every single word that came out of the doctors' mouths. If they said 7-10 days, then, by-God, we would be home in 7-10 days. Right? WRONG!

It wasn't until one of the nurses explained further that we realized that was not realistic. "You see," she said, "the doctors never tell parents about all the more realistic possibilities. Odds are, you will be in here longer than a week. There are hurdles Ty will be presented with that he will have to overcome. It's usually one step forward, then two steps back."

Those words rang through my head, and stuck with me. One step forward, two steps back. It didn't take long to learn that, with Ty, it was more like a half step forward, turn around, fall down, get back up, take two steps back, then, and ONLY THEN, think about taking a step forward. This kid did the hokey-pokey when it came to recovery. It was a constant game of back and forth; one day he was better, the next day he was worse. It messed with my emotions. It tore my soul out and ripped it to shreds, the constant uncertainty of his recovery. I was the kind of person that needed to mentally prepare for everything. I needed to know 2 months ahead of time that I was going out of town, so that I could keep a list of all of the things I would need to bring, and add to it as needed. Here I was, not knowing from minute to minute what may happen. Surely God had made some kind of mistake. Perhaps his GPS had been off, and all of this was meant for a mother who lived down the street from me. One that was more equipped for such uncertainty. I was certainly NOT cut out for this!

*Chapter 16*

# GOING HOME ALONE

W<small>E HOPED AND PRAYED THAT</small> Ty would make a fast recovery, anxious to get him home. At this point, I had been discharged from the hospital. There was no way for us to stay in Ty's PICU room at night, as parents were not allowed to sleep there. The only option was to sleep in the parents' lounge, which was filled with parents nearly piled on top of each other on "not so sanitary" sofas and pull-outs. Travis, a germaphobe, would have no part of this co-habitating lifestyle. We opted to drive home at night, which meant driving over an hour one way, sleeping a few hours, and driving over an hour back to the hospital. It was tiring, but it was worth it to sleep in our own bed.

It was heart-breaking to leave that hospital without him. It was unnatural, and it killed me. Going home to an empty, quiet house. No getting up in the middle of the night with a hungry newborn, no changing diapers. No phone calls from anxious visitors wanting to come by and sneak a peak . . .

Ty was on a ventilator after surgery, but he was being weaned off of it slowly. To be extubated (have the tube taken out of his throat and begin breathing on his own) was the first huge step he would have to take. His medications were slowly being decreased as well, and these were all things he would have to tolerate before going home.

My morning routine was to pick up the phone as soon as I first opened my eyes and call Ty's nurse to get a status report. I would literally keep the phone on the headboard, just inches from my head. As soon as I opened one eye, I would extend my arm and grab that phone. It was as though my arm and my eye were attached to one another. I had a fear that if I were to break that pattern, something bad may happen. (I know, shocking, right?) We would then jump in the shower, and rush to the hospital. I felt a horrible guilt and fear the entire time I was away from him, as though he may need me and I would not be there. I often left the house with wet hair and no makeup, as it would have taken extra time to finish getting ready.

In fact, Travis nearly lost his life one morning by suggesting we stay home long enough for him to mow the lawn before we went to the hospital. Okay, maybe it wasn't quite *that* bad, but I think I nearly had a heart attack by the mere suggestion of such absurdity! I had to get there immediately. There was no time for mowing the lawn. There was hardly time to use the bathroom!

I was finally beginning to feel like he was mine, and being away from him was killing me.

Mother's Day morning was no different. I opened my eyes, picked up the phone and cleared my throat for the first time as it rang. I didn't even take the time to wipe the sleep from my eyes. Our nurse for the day, Jeanne, explained that doctors were preparing to extubate Ty. She said, "How would you like to hold your son without his tube for a Mother's Day gift?" I was ecstatic. I rushed to tell Travis the good news, and we were more eager than ever to get to the hospital. According to Jeanne, they would go ahead and extubate him soon, and when we arrived, we should be able to see him without his tube for the first time since his surgery. I wasn't even sure what he looked like under all of that anymore, and the excitement was more than I could stand!

Every time we pulled into Children's parking garage, I had the same sickening feeling in my stomach. I would walk as fast as possible to the elevator, and Travis would always laugh at me. I could not wait to get inside, although the smell that consumed me when the elevators opened on the 7th floor always made me feel worse. It was as though the smell of the hospital made me even more nervous than I already was. Even after all of this time there, I felt the same way every morning. As we hit the button on the wall to open those big double doors to enter the PICU, another feeling always rushed over me. Within the PICU, there was a different smell. Sort of a sterile, discomforting, hospital smell that was unique from any other area of the hospital. The PICU was shaped like a horseshoe, and the walls were lined with glass doors to individual patient rooms. We were like fish in the pet store, there for the world to see. Like primates being observed by scientists, behind glass, being watched. Or, at least, that's how it felt.

Ty's room was all the way at the end, room 23. We would walk past the desk just inside the doors, down the hall and turn right. Continue down the hall, and turn right again, then, finally, we would be in the home-stretch. It was my routine to stare directly at Ty's door and hope to see his nurse sitting outside in the hall at her desk. We had quickly learned that if the nurse was outside of the room, that was a good sign. As long as he or she was at the desk, that meant Ty was okay and not in direct need of his or her attention. As we would round that last corner every morning, my stomach would knot up as I looked toward that desk. My heart became a lump in my throat, and I struggled with the flash of heat that would start at my gut and work its way up my neck and into my face. Every time. Without fail. The old me would not have been able to recognize this new reality. I had taken my old life so terribly for granted. All of the things I used to find stressful and important now paled in comparison.

This morning, waiting to see Ty without that tube down his throat and taped to his little face, I was so relieved to see Jeanne sitting outside of his door. She stopped us, though, and said she needed to tell us something before we went in and wondered what happened. Ty had been extubated, but that only lasted a few minutes before he had to be re-intubated. It seemed he could not breathe well enough on his own to keep his saturations up. She joked and said she wasn't sure why, but he just wasn't ready. God love that woman. She was so thoughtful, so loving. I'm sure she practiced what she would say to us before we got there, knowing we were so eagerly anticipating such a milestone.

It was a scary time for us. Why was he unable to do this on his own? He did it before the surgery, and he did well with his trial periods of being on room air while being weaned off of the ventilator.

Shortly after this episode, Ty began to run a fever.

It soon became apparent that he had some kind of infection. The arterial line in his wrist, which was used to draw frequent blood gasses, had become infected. The line was removed, and another was put into the other arm. Doctors suspected that this could be the reason for his failure at being extubated. If his body was compromised by the infection, it could have resulted in an inability to sufficiently breathe on his own . . . we prayed that this was the case. There would be no way to know until he recovered a little from the infection and we tried again.

*Chapter 17*

# DOING THE HOKEY-POKEY

WHEN THE DAY CAME THAT Ty was successfully extubated, we were so thrilled. He had had the tube in for so long, his top lip had a little indentation in it from wrapping around the tube. He looked so different without it, after having seen him that way for so long. The tube would come out of his mouth, and a piece of tape was wrapped around the tube then taped above his top lip to keep it in place. After it was gone, he looked like a man who had shaved his moustache. It took a while to get used to looking at him.

By this time, Ty and I had been bonding for a while. It took me several days in the beginning, but he eventually began to feel like he was mine. After he made it through those two surgeries, and I saw what a trooper he was, he began to seem more real to me. We were so proud of his extubation, we went up and down the hallways telling every nurse we knew.

Ty was being fed by this time, but not by mouth because of the tube. He had been given an NG tube, which goes up the nose and down the throat into the stomach. I had begun using a breast pump when he was a couple of days old, and the milk was frozen. The PICU had a special freezer for breast milk, which seemed so strange to me at the time. For whatever reason, though, I was not very successful at pumping. Perhaps it was that I didn't get to hold him regularly, and with the tube, he was unable to cry. My body probably was confused as to where in the world the baby was I was trying to feed, so I was unable to ever get more than an ounce at a time. To make matters more awkward, I had to pump inside of Ty's room. At one time, there had been a pumping room for mothers to use, but because breast milk was a bodily fluid and some had been spilled in the room, the rules changed. I was given a white screen to sit behind, and would have to go and ask the nurse to find the pump everytime I needed it. I would sit in the corner of the room, behind the screen, inside of this room that was nearly all glass. I felt especially bad when we had male nurses because, it never failed, Ty would knock his pulse ox off, and the monitor would sound, and these poor guys would feel uneasy coming in the room with me behind that darned white screen. I'll never forget the sound of that stupid pump as long as I live. Hospital pumps are free-standing on a pole and base, and make a horrible hum as they work. Not only was it terribly painful some days, but the sound of that stupid thing was undeniable. I felt like I should just hang a sign in the hall that said "Hey, I'm in here with my shirt off behind a screen!"

After a few weeks, I got frustrated with pumping. I was getting even less milk now, and even though Ty was being fed only tiny portions of food continuously through his tube, he was having to be supplemented with formula because I could not keep up. I finally quit trying. I felt like a failure in a way, but in another way I was relieved. It was a hard thing to do, having never experienced breast feeding and dealing with that silly pump. I was glad to see that screen get moved out of our room.

Ty began having trouble tolerating his formula. He was being fed probably ¼ what a healthy baby his age would eat, but he was not processing the formula. He began to spit up and have a lot of gas. Luckily, one of our favorite nurses, Janet, was with us that day. She simply had him switched over to soy formula, and that seemed to do the trick. Some of the physicians were suspecting medical problems that would cause the inability to tolerate the food, but Janet started with a simple solution, which worked just fine. I adored her for that. She never got overly excited, which always made us feel at ease. She was loving, kind, and amazing. Tall and very thin, and probably close to our age, I could identify with her. She looked at Ty lovingly, and would make sure he was snuggled nurturingly in his blankets, much like a mother would. She was amazing.

Our little man was now eating, but not much. The pump ran continuously, giving him little drops of formula all day and night. That did not lead to a normal routine by any stretch of the imagination. It was also PICU routine to do baths at night, when nothing was going on. So, he would normally have a bath around 4 am. I was anxious to go home, but not anxious to try and reverse this bizarre schedule he now was accustomed to.

Our next milestone came on a morning I felt would be like every other. By this time, Travis had had to go back to work. I was on my way to the hospital, just minutes away, when my cell phone rang. As I looked at the caller ID screen and saw the hospital's number, my heart pounded. They were given those numbers for emergencies, and now they were calling. I can still feel the nausea I felt as I answered the phone. That heat ran up my neck and into my face and I was beside myself with anxiety. It was our nurse for the day, Carla. We had never had Carla before, but she started by assuring me that everything was okay. I wonder now just how many times she had made calls like this one? She knew to start by saying, "Everything is fine."

She had just called to tell me that Ty would be transferred to "the floor" today. She didn't want me to show up and not be able to find him. Being floored is what you strive for when in the PICU. To be floored is to be moved out of the PICU and into a room out on the floor. This is the final step before going home.

H-O-M-E. The mere thought of that four-letter word was more than I could grasp!

Finally, I could see the light at the end of the tunnel. I called Travis on my way to the hospital and told him the good news. He was sad that he was at work and not there for the big move, but we were both so excited. I rushed inside of that hospital like a freight train. For once, I didn't feel as sick entering the parking garage, or even the PICU. In fact, I think I floated right through those double doors! I victoriously rounded the corner and saw Carla in the hall. What a relief! We were going to the floor.

Within an hour or two, we were out on the floor. We had been told by our PICU nurses that, while it is a big step to go to the floor, it is also harder for parents. PFFFFT! Impossible, I thought! Going to the floor means going home. I could handle it! Right?

In the PICU, Ty had 2 nurses per day, each with a 12 hour shift. While they were on, they had one patient, and that was Ty. The only time that changed was toward the end of our stay in the PICU, when he was less maintenance. Then, if another child came in that required more attention, the nurse may double up. But for the most part, we knew Ty was in good hands, and being monitored closely. On the floor, it would be different. One nurse may have 3 or 4 patients. They may be spread out all over the floor. We would have to stay in his room and care for him for the most part, and the nurse would just oversee things. It would be our job to weigh each diaper, which we had to do to watch for signs of heart failure (in heart failure, a patient will have decreased urine output which would result in swelling of the body). We would not have the luxury of going home at night, or at least it wasn't advised.

To this point, we had not done the normal parental duties. He was, in essence, the hospital's baby, not ours. Or at least that's how it felt. We were just bystanders to the circus that was our son's life, and all that he had known. This strange universe, this scary existence, was becoming 'our normal.'

All that aside, we were ready to go to the floor. Not only was it one step closer to going home, but it was there that we would be allowed to start making Ty familiar with a bottle. We were told a speech therapist would come in and begin working with him to re-teach him how to eat by mouth. All babies are born with this instinct, but if it is not used, it is forgotten. This was something we had never been told about before. In all the preparation we received before Ty was born, we were never told that he would have to be taught to eat. To make matters more complicated, we were told that Downs babies often have a harder time learning because of their sometimes fatter tongues. The thought of giving him a bottle was so exciting. I was ready to go to the floor and get started.

I accompanied our big boy as we went through a new set of double doors just on the other side of the PICU. I had seen these doors every day, from 'our side.' I couldn't believe we were about to walk through them . . . . to 'the other side.'

It was like another universe there. It was not as sterile and cold. It had a warmth about it; even the lighting was different. We had to share a room with another family, which made me uncomfortable. I was used to having a private room, with our own nurse. Ty had developed a horrible case of diaper rash in which he had raw skin with deep spots where he had lost several layers of skin. While this was a minor problem in the PICU, our nurse on the floor chose to quickly address it.

It was almost exciting to see the focus change. If they were worried about clearing up his diaper rash, then they weren't worried about other problems . . . and that was good.

The nurse joked with me and said she had an unconventional way of drying out the rash. She laid him on his stomach (a first) on top of a C shaped Boppy pillow. Over his bed was a very bright, hot light used for procedures. She turned that thing on and let it shine down on his tiny little white butt. She said the heat from the lamp always seemed to dry things up quickly. Ty seemed to like his new positioning, and fell asleep almost immediately. I had never seen him lie on his stomach. I had never seen him uncovered, open to the world, almost, dare I say, 'normal.' It was glorious to be worrying about diaper rash. <u>THIS</u> is what I had been waiting for. I longed to be one of those moms who was terribly upset because her baby had cradle cap or baby acne.

After about an hour, he had his first bowel movement out on the floor. I had been standing right there by his side, reveling in the fact that we were in a regular room, doing seemingly regular things. I stood at attention there beside him, taking it all in.

With no diaper on, I obviously saw everything occur. I noticed that just before he went, he passed some blood and mucus. Assuming it was probably from some intestinal irritation from the antibiotics he had been on, I didn't get too worried, but called the nurse. She didn't seem overly concerned, and let the cardiology team know.

Shortly after, a cardiology resident came in and explained that he felt the blood was caused by the antibiotics as well, but they would do some tests to be sure. I was getting the hang of this! The doctors seemed to agree with *me* - the mom. I could handle this!

It didn't take long for him to come back with a more concerned look on his face. As he knelt there in the floor in front of me, I knew something was wrong. Ty had NEC, Necrotizing EnterColitis, which he explained could be life threatening. There was an opening in the lining of his intestines, which was bleeding. This was detected by X-ray, which showed air in the lining of the intestines. Should this spot rupture, Ty could be in serious danger.

It was like having a glorious dream followed by a horrific nightmare. I had one of my best days and one of my worst days all in one day, and I was alone for the whole thing. As quickly as we had been moved to the floor, we were moved back to the PICU. We got our old room back; we hadn't been gone long enough for it to even be filled. I was so frantic, I called Travis at work immediately. I felt bad, calling him when I knew he would want to leave work but couldn't. I had to call someone, though; I was scared and needed to hear his voice.

No words can truly describe the emotional toll that an experience like this takes on a parent. All of the things that were once important or relevant evaporate into a cloud that represents your old life. Mysteriously, without notice, you are sucked into an unknown land. The primary language there is a foreign one, and you struggle each day just to make sense of the words that swirl around you. The outside world is but a memory, as you are now an 'insider' in a club you never wanted to be in. Like a fraternity pledge being hazed, you are yanked from your comfort zone and forced into compromising situations. Scared, disoriented, alone; you have no choice but to be 'one of them' now.

I recall a time that two of my girlfriends had come to visit, and I opened the door to the parents' lounge to greet them. I found them there, sitting like school girls in the chairs along the wall; feet under their butts in the chairs like they were at recess. They sat there, Starbucks coffees in hand, giggling and telling stories. I stood there in the doorway, observing them, disheveled and unkempt. My hair was not styled, I had on no makeup. I was still wearing maternity clothes, and was bloated and felt terrible about myself. I was disgusted that they had the audacity to act that way in my presence, so happy and smiley. One part of me wanted to lash out at them and tell them to leave, to collapse in the floor in a puddle of emotion and just weep until there were no tears left. The other part of me longed to latch onto them and beg them to take me with them and never look back. I longed to go back to the girl I had been just a year before. I wanted to have my day ruined by a hole in my sock or a speeding ticket.

I wanted to rant and rave all day because the hairdresser took a half inch too much off of my bangs, or because my boss was crabby. It was obvious. I was jealous of them, coffee and all. I didn't expect them to know what to say, or to be able to fix it for me. I just didn't want them to flaunt their 'normal' in my face, either.

*Chapter 18*

# THIS IS <u>NOT</u> WHAT I EXPECTED!

To let the NEC heal, Ty's feedings would be stopped. If there was no food to pass through the intestines, then they would get a break and be able to heal. We had worked so hard to get food into him, and get him to gain even an ounce. Now, we were going to completely deny him of food?

Not only was he not going to be fed, but a horribly large tube was placed down his nose and into his stomach to drain out any stomach secretions as well. It was horrible. This tube filled his entire nostril, and was probably the size of my pinky finger. It was terribly uncomfortable in the back of his throat. He had just begun to cry at a normal volume after being intubated for so long, and now he had something else in his throat.

As a mother, it is so painful to have these things happen to your child against your will. There was nothing I could do; he had to have this done. It was difficult to comfort him as he lay there in a bed. I held him occasionally, but it was difficult to do with so many wires and things attached to him. How much I got to hold him also depended on what nurse we had. Some nurses did not seem very comfortable with our holding him, as though we would pull something loose. They would limit our holding time, while other nurses would let us hold him all day. At this point, we had only changed a few diapers, and had only bathed him once, with assistance in the NICU when he was a day old. We weren't exactly parents, we felt, because we hadn't done the parental things yet. We were biological parents, yes, but not parents in the active sense.

That tube was tough to get used to. It was so big that it was not very flexible, and tugged on his little face no matter how we taped it. It extracted any stomach secretions he had, which were green and foul smelling. He was unable to be fed for over a week, but was so sick he didn't seem to really notice.

After several days in the PICU under "NEC watch," we got moved back to the floor. Once again, Travis was at work when this happened and was heartbroken. I found out this time when I made my morning call and spoke to nurse Beckah, whom we really liked. She told me that by the time I would get there, he may be moved. I didn't care, I told her to move him as soon as possible.

He was still in the PICU when I got there, but not for long. We made our glorious ascension to 'the floor', and once again, we shared a room. This time our room partner was a little girl about 7 years old named Brandy, who also had cardiac problems. She, however, was much worse off. She was in heart failure, and would probably need a transplant soon. She was on the transplant list, but the doctors preferred to keep her heart in as long as possible. It was disturbing to see her. She represented what Ty would eventually become. She was our future, in living form. Her lips were blue, a common thing in heart failure. She was old enough to know what was going on, and she hated it in the hospital. She would be going home soon, but she was not very cooperative with nurses, doctors, or even her mother. Who could blame her? She had been a human pin cushion for her entire life. She was entitled to be a little grumpy.

That first night, Travis and I both stayed in the room. We shared a chair that pulled out into a one person bed. This meant that we both laid on our sides, our bodies squished together between the arms of this chair. It seemed as though one of us needed to roll over every 20 minutes, which meant the other person had to sit up and scoot over until the rearranging was done. Needless to say, it did not make for a restful night's sleep. On top of that, Brandy was not very cooperative. She had a PICC line in her arm at the fold, as did Ty. This line went through the arm and up to the heart, and gave doctors and nurses valuable information about the heart's status. Ty had an arm board on, which kept his arm straight so that he could not bend it. Brandy, however, did not have one because she was old enough to keep her arm straight. However, she did not do that. All night long, she would bend her arm. When she did, the monitor would sound. The alarm was loud, and every time her mother would tell her, "Brandy, straighten out your arm." She would, for a few minutes, but then it would happen again. When she wasn't bending her arm, her medication pumps would beep. She had been on several medicines, which were put into pumps and ran through an IV. When one of these medications would get low, the pump would give a warning beep to alert nurses. Because we were no longer in the PICU, though, the nurse did not hear it. Therefore, her mother would have to call the nurse every time and let her know. It never seemed to fail that the nurses would not respond quickly enough, and the pump would run completely out of medication. Then it would beep continuously until they came in and reset it.

All night long, we listened to Brandy's monitors, her mother yelling at her, and flipped and flopped in that chair.

By morning, we were ready to move. Brandy was not very friendly to any doctors or nurses. That was understandable, given her age and all she had been through. However, it did not make for a great living environment since we were only separated by a curtain. Fortunately, we were later moved to our own room, where we could sleep on a fold out window seat which was more our size. Never had I imagined I would be thankful to sleep in a window seat . . . but I was!

By this time, Ty was getting healthier, and started to notice he was not being fed. The last few days of his fasting were pretty hard for all three of us. He cried a lot, which he had never done before. He was hungry and fussy, and did not want the tube in his nose any more. We often had to keep his arms restrained or tucked under a blanket to keep him from pulling at it. That was a hard thing to do as parents, to keep him so tightly tucked in when he wanted to move freely. He was finally starting to act like a 'regular' baby, and we were holding him back. It was heart-wrenching, but necessary. That seemed to be a common theme for us at this point.

## Chapter 19

# PRAYING FOR POOP!

IT DOESN'T TAKE LONG WITH a sick child to learn that sometimes it's the little things in life that make you the happiest. For us, it was when Ty had his first tiny bowel movement since his fasting. We had been told to watch for this, because it would be a sign that his intestines were healed. At this point, whatever we had to do to feel 'normal' was welcome, even if it was praying for poop!

Though he had not eaten, there would be enough stomach secretions that slipped through to form a small movement. We were thrilled to call the nurse in to look at this tiny speck in a diaper. She checked it for blood, and the test was negative. There was no blood! This was a wonderful sign. Cardiologists wanted to wait another day or so before feeding him, just to be safe.

When Ty finally got fed, it was in a different way. He still had the NG tube, but this time he did not get a pump. He was fed "bolus" feedings, which meant he was fed every few hours through the tube, but it was done manually. The nurses would come in and remove the plunger from a large syringe. They would then attach the syringe to the tube, and pour the formula into the syringe. The flow of the food was determined by how high the syringe was held. They were unable to hold it too high, as it would give him too much food and he would gag. That was another heart-wrenching sight.

For the first few feedings, the nurses handled everything. At this point, we had never fed our son. Finally, they told us that we would need to learn how to give him the bolus feeds. We were confused, because we thought he was going to learn to use a bottle. This was apparently another myth the doctors had led us to believe, which the nurses let us in on. They explained that most cardiac kids go home with an NG tube, and it is the parents' job to teach them to eat at home. According to the nurses, the doctors are not concerned with teaching the kids to eat. They let that wait until later.

Although I understood that *how* he ate was not all that important to them, it was important to us. That was just one more thing he did not do normally, yet. It was uncomfortable for him to have that tube down the back of his throat, even though it was small. He would gag a lot, especially if we moved him. Also, though it sounds superficial, we just wanted him to eat like every other kid. We were not prepared for something so controversial as feeding him this way. The tube remained in at all times, and just got changed about once a week. It was taped to his face, which caused a lot of redness and irritation. He also liked to grab it and pull on it, which would not be pleasant for him should he get it loose and pull it out.

We fed him for the first time, and it was a little scary. If we held the syringe up too high, he gagged. Once we got it to a comfortable level, it would take anywhere from 30 minutes to an hour for him to eat. We were at the mercy of gravity, and that was not easy. By the time he was done eating, we had about 2 hours until we needed to feed him again. It was strange. We just always planned on waiting for him to cry, and sticking a bottle in his mouth. With this method, he would get hungry, but then it would take about 15 minutes for his stomach to begin to feel full and then he would calm down. With other kids, they were comforted by the feeling of the bottle in their mouth; they associated it with relief. With Ty, he knew no relief until his stomach felt fuller. It was hard, but we were happy to finally do something parent-like.

Because Ty hadn't eaten for about 10 days, his stomach had shrunk tremendously. We had to start out with small amounts of food, and work our way up each time. In the beginning, he got less than a tablespoon of food. He eventually worked his way up a little, but was still receiving much less food than a healthy baby. Because of this, he received formula that was mixed more concentrated to give him more calories.

We were past our big hurdles, and were so thankful. I prayed every day, and made sure to thank God for helping us through our hard times and for keeping Ty healthy.

*Chapter 20*

# TRYING TIMES

TY HAD LOST A CONSIDERABLE amount of weight from not eating, and slowly gained a few ounces. There were so many other routines we never anticipated, like nurses coming in every couple of hours to check his blood pressure. He hated this, and would normally get upset, making his blood pressure rise. It was not a fun game to him. Also, he had to be weighed every morning to monitor his growth. Unfortunately, the ladies that brought the scales around could wait no later than 6am to do so. Every morning, they would come and wake that poor baby up to weigh him. They would strip him naked and lay him on that scale, which seemed so barbaric. Often, he had just gotten to sleep when they would come in, pushing the scale into the door and wall causing a commotion, and rip his clothes off. It was little things like this that had gotten us to the point of being fed up. The nurses in the PICU were right, THE FLOOR WAS NOT A PLEASANT PLACE TO BE! It felt as though they had forgotten he was just a baby, and that we were new parents. We slept there, of course, if that's what you want to call it. The nurses came in all night checking his blood pressure, fiddling with his monitors, and swapping out his medications. Often, they would not hear the pumps beep when his meds got low, and we would wake up and have to call them to come in. Then they would beep again when they were empty, and we would have to remind them to come in. We were thrilled to be so close to going home, but fed up with the "service" we got from most of the nurses. We had a few that we adored, and it was such a relief when they worked. Some, however, left much to be desired. In one incident, I nearly lost my cool. Ty had been on 3 different antibiotics to fight the NEC, and was nearing the end of the cycle on them. Each syringe would be tagged with a label with Ty's name and information, to avoid any mixup. I knew the names of all the meds he received, and most nurses would tell me what they were giving him whenever they came in. One day, though, we had a new nurse. She came in with a syringe in her hand and began to place it in the pump. I asked her what it was, and she spewed out a name I did not recognize. I asked her if that was a new med, as it was not one of his regulars. She looked at me as though I was annoying her, and rattled off another common name for the drug. Still not identifying it, I asked her if she was sure about what she was doing. She looked down at the syringe, and casually excused herself for a moment. When she came back, she just as casually told me that the med she had almost given Ty was not even his. She blew it off, and started the correct antibiotic. I was furious. What if he had been allergic to that medication? What if it interacted with the others he was on? What was that medication even used for? It could have killed him! Had I not been there, she never would have even looked at the label on the syringe. I was appalled by her ability to write this mistake off and act as though it was a minor accident. From that day on, we never left Ty's room unless we had a nurse that we knew very, very well. Even then, we only left to go to the cafeteria, or to attend church on Sunday morning.

## Chapter 21

# DADDY'S LITTLE BOY

ONE DAY, OUT OF THE blue, our nurse Nicki asked us if we wanted to help bathe Ty. Was she kidding? Of course we wanted to help! This was only the second or third time we had been able to do this, and even then we were spectators more than anything. It was then that we reached another milestone with Ty . . . big boy clothes. Like I said before, it was really the little things that were so exciting for us. Nicki asked us if we had any clothes with us. Of course we did. We had brought a diaper bag packed with clothes and every other luxury when I went into labor. It had remained faithfully in the truck for weeks along with his car seat. Until this point, for 4 ½ weeks, he had never worn clothes. He was simply wrapped in a blanket, or once in a while wore a lovely, white hospital t-shirt.

This was a silly milestone, but it was exciting to us. We had never seen our son in clothes before. Travis raced to the parking garage to fetch that diaper bag. We rejoiced at the thought of this sight, and were anxious to play dress up!

We quickly learned that at just a little over 7 pounds, he did not fit into anything we brought for him. The neck on that onesie hung off of his shoulders, and he looked rather ridiculous, but we didn't care. He looked like a teenage girl in the 80's, his shirt hanging off of his shoulders. All he needed was some leg warmers and a side ponytail, and he would have been set!

Travis even went home at some point and brought back a sleeper he had been dying to put on Ty since I was about 6 months pregnant. It had been purchased during one of our many shopping sprees, and poor Travis had been waiting patiently for this moment. It was white with blue trim, and was covered with little puppies. Scattered here and there on the garment were the words "Daddy's little boy." Travis glowed as he put that sleeper on his son, even though it was a little big.

We were nearing the end of the list of accomplishments Ty had to make before he went home. He was now eating, and gaining a tiny bit of weight. He was having bowel movements, and was doing pretty well. The goal with his feeding was to get him to eat 70cc in one sitting. Though this was only about 2 ounces, it was a lot for a baby who had been starved until the day before. Those 70cc's took forever to choke down, and he was full to the brim. He gagged a lot, and we could tell he was uncomfortable. We had done it, though; we got up to their requirements.

A nurse had been in to discuss again the signs and symptoms of heart failure. She explained that we should always keep an eye on his color, his breathing, and watch for swelling, especially in the face. Now, I had been noticing for about 2 days that Ty's cheeks seemed unusually fat, and had been concerned. Still feeling more like an observer than a mother, though, I struggled with whether or not to bring it up. When I finally pointed it out to her, she just laughed and said she thought that was because he was finally filling out, and that I shouldn't be concerned. She said that usually the swelling we should watch for would occur more around the eye area. With that, I tried to forget my worries, but still felt a little uneasy about his newly fat face.

Again, I should have followed my gut instinct. But, caught up in the moment of hitting milestones, and not wanting to take another step backward, I stifled the feeling I had in my heart. We were closer than ever to going home, and I was ready!

*Chapter 22*

# A FAMILY IS BORN

I'LL NEVER FORGET WHEN A case worker from the hospital came into our room. She wanted to go over a few things with me, and give me names of pediatricians and set up some follow-up appointments with cardiologists. When she introduced herself, she said she was there to make a few arrangements before we got ready to go home.

GULP! I'm sorry, what? Go home? Could it be? We were getting close, and we were ready.

On Friday, June 8th, we were told that we would probably go home by Monday. To hear the word HOME come from someone's mouth again was breathtaking. Until now, that was just an unattainable goal, kind of like winning the lottery. We all hear people talk about what they would buy if they won the lottery, but we all know that the odds of that happening are about a bazillion to one. This woman, who walked so non-challantly into our room, had carried with her a winning lottery ticket!

We joyfully called our parents to let them know that we were in the homestretch. Later that morning, our nurse came in and said that we may be going home as soon as Saturday. "That's tomorrow," we said. She smiled and said she wasn't sure yet, but she thought she had overheard someone say something about Saturday. Needless to say, we were speechless. We may be about to spend our final night in the hospital!

By this time, it was about 9:30am, and I had just gone to the cafeteria to get breakfast. I brought it back to the room, and sat it on the table. We were just starting to open the boxes of cafeteria food when one of the residents came into our room. She opened her mouth, and blurted out the most astonishing question imaginable: 'How would you like to go home today?' We nearly choked as she said it, and I'm pretty sure all color drained from my face as my jaw hit the ground. It felt a little rushed, but we weren't going to argue. She said there were a few more things to take care of, and then we could probably just go home.

To this day, I question the rushed nature of this decision. Had our insurance stopped paying? Was there a snafoo someplace that we were unaware of? Until now, we were still facing a mountain of 'To-Do's' that had to be accomplished. Suddenly, without warning, we were hearing the words Ty and Home in the same sentence!

We were unable to eat our breakfast, now. We looked at Ty, and could not believe he might be ours soon. Shortly after this unbelievable news, a nurse and someone from cardiology came into the room. They were going to remove Ty's PICC line. This was something he had had from the very beginning. As I explained before, it ran up his arm and to his heart. They very delicately removed the PICC line, which was stitched into place and taped many times. It was strange to see that part of his arm, which had always been covered.

It seemed like only minutes until a nurse came in.

She lowered the side of Ty's bed, and began removing all of the leads from his chest. She unhooked his pulse ox, and even his IV. She picked him up, and for the first time, he was not attached to any type of machine. I had never, EVER, seen him like this. The first time I ever laid eyes on him, he was in an incubator, being bagged. We had never been able to walk freely with him before. We had never been able to get further than 3 feet from his bed before. Suddenly, he was free. She handed him to us, and told us that we could go for a walk. "In fact," she said, "he has some prescriptions to be filled down at the pharmacy before you go home. Why don't you take him down there and get them?" Did she just give us the okay to take him out of the room, and down to the main floor to the pharmacy? Alone? Just the 3 of us?

Like a child allowed to ride their bike down the street alone for the first time, we jumped at the chance, and nearly ran to the elevators. We went down to the pharmacy, our first walk as a family. We had never been alone with our son, away from a hospital room before. It was a little scary, quite honestly. We had become so dependent on the monitors to tell us he was okay, and on having a nurse right there at our disposal. Here we were, alone, on an elevator. Just the three of us!

On our way back to the room, we stopped by the PICU. We took a walk that was similar to a NASCAR victory lap through the PICU, telling everyone that we were going home. The looks we got as we carried a cord-free, monitor-free, everything-free Ty were memorable.

It was all happening so fast; we were in a whirlwind. That Friday morning, when cardiology made their regular rounds at 6 am, the surgeon said nothing about us going home that day. He did mention that we may go home soon, but he never let on that it would be this soon. The resident that came in and delivered the good news was a woman we were hardly familiar with. Part of both of us wondered if our surgeon, Dr. Huddleston, even knew that they were sending us home. We ignored that fear, though, figuring surely he would have to approve the orders to send us home. He was a man of few words, and we just assumed that he didn't want to get our hopes up.

We waited a while in our room for all of the arrangements to be completed. Travis did something he had been waiting to do, take all of our belongings to the truck. By this time, we had accumulated a ton of stuff in our room, and he had to make several trips. When he returned, he was carrying Ty's car seat. It looked so strange to see him carry that thing through the door. Until now, it had done nothing but decorate the back seat. Now, there it was, sitting on the table, just waiting to be filled. Were we dreaming?

Soon after Travis packed the car, we were free to go. We loaded Ty into his bright yellow and blue car seat, and off we went. It was so awkward to just walk out the door with him. We had lived in fear for so long, and now we were leaving. No one escorted us to the front of the hospital. We were just handed some paperwork, and sent on our way. It was one of the strangest feelings I have ever experienced . . . freedom.

We nearly floated to the parking garage. As we rode the elevator up to our level, we could do nothing but stare at each other in awe. As we walked to our Explorer, as we had done every night, something was different. We would not be coming back in the morning. We would no longer search for a parking spot, anxious to get inside of the hospital. We were going home. This was the best day of my life, and still is. It was June 8, 2001 . . . Ty was 6 weeks old.

*Chapter 23*

# AND THEN THERE WERE THREE!

ARRIVING AT HOME AS A family, rather than a couple, was so amazing. We were beside ourselves as we introduced our magnificent son to his new surroundings. What was he thinking? The smell, the quiet, the calm . . . all so new to him. Frankly, it was like new to us after spending every waking moment by his side. New felt SO good.

It actually took a few days for the smell of the hospital to fully leave him. I know that that sounds crazy, but between the sterile PICU aroma that I can still smell if I close my eyes, and the smell he gave off from the medications he was on – he had not yet smelled like a baby other than the couple of times we gave him a sponge bath and lathered him with that yummy pink lotion. Even then, the smell did not last long. But now, at home with us where he belonged, he began to look like, smell like, feel like a baby. He was no longer a patient, no longer a number, no longer a stranger to his parents. We were finally learning the ins and outs of Ty Allen Naeger. It was an experience. We were so new at parenting. Everything had been done for us until that point, and Ty was not your average baby. Just the fact that he was fully portable was fascinating to us. We spent a lot of time just carrying him around the house, enjoying the fact that we could take him anywhere . . . so different from the 2-foot leash of wires he had just hours before.

We looked so forward to taking him to church, his first introduction to the world. There we sat, in the pew, where we had sat so many times before. This time was different, though. We were accompanied by a diaper bag, and a beautiful son. We had wanted his first outing to be perfect. We wanted him to look nice, but he was so small, we could find only onesies to fit him. The poor little guy spent his first day in church sporting nothing but a onesie and little denim tennis shoes that were way too big. Luckily, it was chilly in church, so he was covered from the waist down with a blanket - - that helped disguise his little naked legs! Even after all this time of eagerly anticipating this moment, we were still ill-prepared. We didn't care, though, naked legs or not, he was ours!

*Chapter 24*

# HAPPY, NERVOUS FAMILY

WE WERE SO HAPPY TO be a family, yet so nervous of every little thing. It is hard to let down your guard when you've lived in fear for so long. Every noise he made scared me. Every face he made had me wondering if he was in pain. I'll never forget the way he looked in his swing. He loved his swing. Unfortunately, the blue and tan plaid seat made a reflection off of his skin that left him looking a terrible color. For a normal baby, with normal parents, this would probably go unnoticed. However, for the paranoid family living in our home, every ride in the swing left me in fear of him being sick. One of the things we were to watch was his coloring. A change in skin tone could mean many things, including heart failure. So, of course I took that warning to the extreme and spent his leisurely swinging escapades in utter fear as I stared at him endlessly. I watched him as closely as you would watch the television during the juiciest part of your favorite show.

Of course, we also watched his breathing. I'm surprised the poor boy didn't catch pneumonia from me freezing him lifting his shirt every 5 minutes to see if his breathing seemed labored. Labored breathing, of course, was a sign of heart failure. It's funny, but every normal baby behavior can also be a sign of heart failure. Persistent crying, change in skin color, labored breathing, lethargy . . . . you know, all the stuff normal newborns do from time to time . . . . yeah, they told me all the things to watch for, but they never told me how to decipher whether it was normal baby stuff or heart failure. This kid really should have come with an Owner's Manual!

We did, however, have some help watching for the big concerns. We now had a home health nurse that came in once every other week in the beginning. She would check his O2 Sats, listen to his heart, and weigh him. I was so thrilled when he had gained just an ounce or two, not knowing that a healthy child would gain up to a pound every couple of weeks. For us, a couple of ounces was reason to celebrate. On alternating weeks, we drove over an hour to return to Children's Hospital to see the cardiologist. Then, throw in a couple of visits to the pediatrician a month—we were well supervised.

We were approaching our one month anniversary of coming home. We had made it a whole month. We had an appointment with the cardiologist at 11am. My dear friend since high school, Shelley, an RN in the Navy, had been in town visiting from Virginia, and volunteered to tag along. The ride to the hospital would have been tough for me without someone riding along. I worried so much about my little monkey being in the back seat, especially since he faced the rear. There was no way for me to see him, no way for me to fret over his color, breathing and overall health if I couldn't see him.

As we arrived at the hospital, I had no worries. I had my beautiful boy with me, my dearest friend by my side, and life was good! Shelley, Ty and I went into the cardiologist's office and expected to have a short trip.

It didn't take long for Dr. Hirsch to blow me out of the water on the idea of a quick in and out visit. "You're going to kill me," he said in his South African accent. My heart pounded, my stomach flipped, and I waited for the end of the sentence. He proceeded to tell me that Ty was in heart failure. He had gained little or no weight, and his heart was enlarged, meaning it was working too hard. It's interesting, actually. Just as any muscle that is worked beyond it's normal capacity, the heart will enlarge when put under strain.

Dr. Hirsch assured me that the failure was not severe, yet, but that it did need immediate attention. He proceeded to explain that Ty was retaining fluid, a definite sign of heart failure. He would be admitted to the hospital for the weekend and given doses of Lasix to rid him of the water he was retaining. His medication dosages would be altered, and he should be free to go home by Monday.

I was furious! Not at Dr. Hirsch, but at myself. Myself, and that nurse!! THAT nurse, the one that argued with me about Ty looking puffy! I knew in my heart before we left the hospital the first time that Ty did not look like himself. Wanting to believe I was wrong, I trusted the nurse when she laughed off my concerns about his puffy cheeks.

I was heartbroken that I did not know in advance that there was a problem. Other than the puffiness in his face, he seemed fine. Dr. Hirsch explained that Ty had not gained weight because his body was burning every calorie he took in just to function because of his heart's inefficiency. By reducing the water retention and increasing the amount of diuretics he would be given daily, we could hopefully get him to gain weight. Not what I wanted to hear, but not the worst diagnosis possible, either.

I frantically called Travis at work. I was so devastated to think of being in that dreaded hospital again. We had just gotten home, and gotten settled. It's funny, but when he was in the hospital the first time, I knew no different. I had never cared for him alone, and didn't fully grasp the reality of him being mine. But now we had routines. We were getting comfortable at home, and I was used to doing everything for him. I was accustomed to feeding him, giving him his meds twice a day, and all the things I needed to do. And now I would have to turn over my mothering to the nurses again. It was very hard to let go of that. But, I did.

The weekend went well, I suppose. He came home weighing only 6 ½ pounds, an amazing 10 ounces lighter than he went in. That was devastating, as all the weight I thought I had worked to get him to gain was only water. He was now smaller than he was when he was born.

Life went on, and he slowly gained a few ounces here and there. He seemed to be doing better, and feeling a little better. After struggling with insurance companies for the past 5 weeks, I finally got Ty a speech therapist. It's an odd thing, but it appears that someone dropped the ball when it came to Ty's feedings. He was sent home with a feeding tube, and I was told he would receive therapy to learn to feed by mouth. However, we never got a therapist to help with that. I called several offices through the hospital, and fought with my insurance company until I was blue in the face. Finally, Holly was assigned to Ty's case. She was very nice, and worked hard to get Ty used to having things in his mouth. It seemed odd to parents of healthy children, but Ty had no instinct to suck, and never put things into his mouth. He gagged when something touched his tongue, and Holly assured me that, with work, he would learn to drink from a bottle.

We now had a home health nurse 2 days a week on the weeks that we did not see the cardiologist or pediatrician. We also had occupational/ physical therapy to help Ty become more limber and learn to support his own head, something he absolutely could not do. Now, we added speech therapy to the mix twice a week. Our house was constantly being visited by someone, and on the quiet days, we were packing up to drive over an hour to one of our doctor's appointments. Things were hectic, but wonderful.

At the time, at my ripe old age of 24, I couldn't understand why our family marveled at us. They were shocked at how well we handled all that was thrown at us, and I just couldn't understand why. Now, at 34 years of age, my brother is about to turn 24. I look at him, and where he is in his life, and, for the first time, I can see him the way everyone else saw us. I can't imagine watching Marty go through this, unable to fix it for him. I can't imagine how my heart would break for him, and how proud I would be as he handled it. I can finally see just how much of the load God carried for me, walking by my side. He carried most of the bags, and I just took turns carrying one at a time. God got me through . . . I see that now.

Ty loved to sit in his bouncy seat and just be talked to. He also preferred to be held out in front of you, facing you, rather than being held like a baby. Even when sitting down, we would put our feet up on the coffee table and let him lean against our thighs so that he could look us straight in the face. That's what made him happy. He was very opinionated. He was little trouble, really. He didn't cry much, unless he was hungry or had a dirty diaper. Oh, how could I forget? He also cried at bath time. He hated the bath. Other than that, he was a breeze. He was far behind other babies his age. He was not able to hold up his head, made little noise, and was very, very small. Yet, somehow, we did not see those things then. We had nothing to compare him to, and he was OURS. He was alive, and he was ours, and he was PERFECT.

Seeing how Ty was progressing, and how attached I was to him; I realized I had a big decision to make. On July 25, 2001, I turned in my letter of resignation to the Ambulance District's Board of Administrators, effective August 8. I was so sad to leave, but so happy to do so for Ty. It was a bitter sweet letter, because those men were my family. I loved them as much as I loved my family, and it was going to be tough to turn that page in my life.

On July 27, 2001 we had another routine visit with the cardiologist. I have to admit, I was scared to death this time. Ty had been looking much better. His coloring had been wonderful, actually. In fact, at times I worried because he looked "too pink." I held my breath as the appointment began, scared of what may unfold. When Dr. Hirsch saw him, he agreed with me that he was indeed pink, and reassured me that pink was good. He laughed and spoke directly to Ty telling him to keep up the good work. Was I ever relieved! My fears were calmed when he gave Ty the okay to go home. I couldn't help but become overjoyed, and I told him I could just kiss him for the good news. He blushed a little and laughed. I honestly think at that moment, I probably could have laid a big kiss right on his cheek. I could breathe again. We could go home.

Dr. Hirsch was such a nice man. Very soft spoken, very genuine. He always remembered my name, spoke to me as an equal, and made me feel so confident in his abilities. I knew in my heart that I had placed my child in competent hands. I was, and still am, so thankful that he had chosen to come to St. Louis from South Africa to help children like Ty. He was truly sent by God, I believe.

*Chapter 25*

# UNCONDITIONAL LOVE

TY LED A SOMEWHAT SHELTERED life, I suppose. Scared that he would get sick, we did not go many places with him. We did, however, always take him to church, where he was a perfect angel. He went to the store with me a few times to pick up formula, and other than that, the only outings he attended were family functions. In the short few weeks we had been home, he had attended several birthday parties for his cousins. For so long, the youngest 10 of his cousins waited patiently to see this "Baby Ty" fellow they had heard so much about. They would come to the hospital to visit, although they were never allowed into his room. I used to laugh that they probably did not believe that there actually was a baby Ty, (since they had never seen him) and probably thought that their parents were leaving them in the hospital cafeteria and having a party somewhere.

So, once we came home, I tried to take Ty to every family event to get the kids acquainted with him. They were wonderful, and as small as they were, they all seemed to have an understanding that Ty was very special. They had waited so long for him to come home, and many of them would hold him and talk to him. I explained to the older kids (ages 4-9) why he had a tube in his nose, and why I had to put his milk in it instead of in his mouth. I showed them how I used the stethoscope to check the tube placement, and let them listen to his stomach as I put air through the tube so that they could hear what I was listening for. They were fascinated, and that was all the explanation they needed. They saw no flaws in him, no reason to be scared of him. He was baby Ty, and they loved him.

Once, in the grocery store, I saw a little girl about 5 years old looking very closely at his feeding tube. I smiled at her, hoping she would not be frightened. She, in turn, came up to me and asked me what was in his nose. I answered her "Well, it looks sort of like a piece of spaghetti, doesn't it?" I went on to tell her he had to use that to drink his milk, because he was sick. She just looked at me, and said "Oh!", and went on about her business. It was fun to watch the kids, with all their innocence, stare at him for a minute, and then just accept him as one of their own. His cousins had grown to love him so much that they could not concentrate sometimes on their surroundings, as they were so busy talking to Ty. I looked forward to the role Ty would play in his cousins' acceptance of other kids with disabilities. I trusted that one reason Ty was sent to us in this package was to teach his cousins to love all people, and to never judge by looks or handicaps. So far, they were all passing the test with flying colors.

*Chapter 26*

# ANGEL ENCOUNTER

As August began, we were approaching another cardiac catheterization to evaluate Ty's heart function. The outcome of this test would determine when his next operation would be. On August 3, we went to yet another cousin's birthday party. All was well, and it was nice to be out and about. We were pretty darn close to a 'normal' family now, going to birthday parties. What a wonderful feeling!

We had been told about a healing mass to be held on Monday, August 6th in Farmington. We felt that perhaps it being held so close to our home was a sign that we should take Ty and have him prayed for. In fact, our speech therapist, Holly, also planned to attend after hearing about it from another patient's family.

On Monday night, we entered the school gymnasium where the healing mass was being held. It was a full house, nothing but a sea of heads covering the floor. Looking for a place to sit, a hand gently touched my shoulder. A kind man who had seen us enter led us to an aisle and brought us two chairs. We were near the back of the gym, but at least we were there. It was hot with so many people in such a small space, in fact, there were people standing all around the perimeter of the room.

Seated in front of us was a young girl whom I would guess to be about 11 or 12. She was a beautiful girl, seated next to her mother. Her beauty was not only external, but poured from the eyes that peaked out from under a floppy hat. She had no hair, and was so frail and thin that she sometimes laid over on her mother in pure exhaustion. As sick as she obviously was, she could not hold back a smile as she turned around time and time again to gaze at Ty. She would look at him almost as if she could see into his soul. She would pull her mother's sleeve and tell her, "Look at him, Mom, isn't he so cute?" I remember thinking to myself, how does she even know he is a boy? He was not dressed in blue . . . but yet she seemed to *know* him in a way that I still do not understand. The two of them held a conversation with their eyes throughout the healing mass, which lasted several hours. I wanted so badly to talk to her, but could not find the words. To this day, I can see her when I close my eyes, and wonder what became of her. There is a part of me that thinks she was an angel. There was something about her that moved me. Though she was weak and obviously ill, she seemed to glow as she and Ty exchanged glances. There was more to it than just a little girl looking at a baby . . . . I just know there was.

When the time finally came to go to the front of the gymnasium to receive a blessing, we realized that the crowd was to go up row by row, starting in the front. As we sat at the back of the gym, we wondered just how long it would be, as Ty had already been stripped down to just a onesie and was still hot. Just then, a man with a gentle face came and led us to the front of the line. He seemed to know we needed this blessing, and Ty was just too small to wait in line. We nervously stood in the front of the gym as the priest came down the line. When he got to Ty, he looked at him with love and kindness in his eyes and asked, "Does he have problems with his lungs?" Confused, we answered, "No, Father, he has a bad heart and needs a healing."

He placed his hand so gently on Ty's forehead, and prayed for God to be with him and help him. As we exited the line, we met up with Ty's grandparents and a few family friends that had also been at the mass.

Talking in the school kitchen, which was much cooler, we were amazed at how many people approached us and asked for Ty's name so that they could pray for him. It was as though they were drawn to us. Many did not even ask what was wrong with him, they just held our hands with such sincerity and assured us that he would be in their prayers. In a room of at least a thousand people, many sick and many children . . . Ty had somehow gotten their attention.

We were relieved when we left there that night. Our hearts were warmed to see how many people offered their prayers, and we knew God was there that night. He knew that we were there, and He knew we trusted that He would be with Ty and take care of him.

On Tuesday, Ty weighed in at 7 pounds, 10 ounces. He was gaining weight slowly but surely, and I was thrilled when the home health nurse read the scale. He seemed to be doing well, and we were confident as we approached Friday's cardiac cath. That afternoon, as he enjoyed his swing, he did something unusual. Ty spent much of his time with his head turned toward his right. He had spent a lot of time that way when he was on the vent in the hospital, and that was something we had been trying to correct with physical therapy. But today, as he sat in his swing, he looked toward his left. He seemed to see something there, it was as though he were looking at something. I joked with him, and asked him if he was looking at the angels. To this day I think that is what he was doing. There was just something about the way he looked. He was not just looking, he was ***looking***.

On Wednesday, we experienced something amazing. As we sat on the couch, as a family, watching a television show . . . something made Travis and me laugh. As we laughed, we heard a sound we had never heard before—a third laugh. We looked down at Ty, who was seated comfortably on my lap, as usual – and saw him chuckling, as though he were imitating us. What a milestone! We could not wait to tell everyone what he had done. He *was* a real baby. He *did* do baby things. We were so thrilled, so proud, and so sure that he was on the path to getting well. That was a day that I will never forget.

The days of that week were speeding by, and soon it would be time to go back to the hospital. The schedule was that on Friday morning, Ty would undergo the cardiac cath. After he regained consciousness and ate, he would be allowed to go home, just in time for my 25th birthday on Saturday, August 11.

*Chapter 27*

# IN THE PRESENCE OF THE HOLY SPIRIT

W E RECEIVED A TELEPHONE CALL that week to move the cath up one day to August 9th---a change I welcomed as I anticipated my first birthday as a mother. We were still filled with comfort and confidence since the healing mass. Travis took the day off of work and we left bright and early Thursday morning to head to the hospital. In the back of my mind, I wondered if the cardiac cath would leave doctors boggled. I prayed that they would return with the amazing information that his heart was doing wonderfully, and another surgery may not be necessary. We had been filled with such peace since Monday's mass, and for the first time I was not nervous about heading to the hospital.

On the way to Children's that morning, I had my first encounter with the scent of roses. It is said that when the Holy Spirit is nearby, an overwhelming scent of fresh roses is sometimes present. As I sat in the back seat of our Explorer, staring down at my beautiful son, I smelled them. At first, I was not sure what I smelled. I asked Travis, "Do you smell that?" He looked at me as though I were crazy, and asked me what I was talking about. "Flowers," I said, "I smell flowers. Roses. As though the back of the truck were full of them. You don't smell that?" As I looked at his reflection in the rear-view mirror, I could read his smile by the gleam in his eyes. We both knew what I was smelling, and that strengthened our peace in what would unfold that day. I was convinced that God had provided me with this as confirmation that all was well, and going according to plan.

We arrived at the hospital, and had to wait several hours for the procedure. Ty had not eaten in hours in preparation for the cath, and he was getting hungry. We had a room in the PICU, since he would be observed there after the procedure. I remember the joy I felt because for the first time as we sat behind the glass of that PICU room . . . I did not feel like a specimen. For once, we were not there because Ty was gravely ill . . . we were only in the PICU so that he would have a room after his procedure was through. His nurse rarely came into the room, which was a change of pace from the hustle and bustle that used to fill his PICU room. She even came in once and said, "Let me know if you need anything. I'm trying not to treat him like a patient, so I'll be at my desk."

Ty looked so handsome these days. He had never lost any hair, and it was such a perfect length on the sides that it had the nurse asking if he had had a haircut. He laid there like a little grown up, watching his mobile and being so good. I worried that he would be hungry, but he was so content. The day was going so well, and my friend Mary, who had been with me when I went into labor, even stopped in to say hello. I remember her bringing me a baby backpack that I could borrow to put Ty in, so that I could take him places without carrying his car seat. She told Ty how handsome he looked, and gave him a kiss on his head. I can still see her leaning in to kiss him, and can still recall the pattern on the backpack that she brought. I was so grateful that she stopped by, and that she treated Ty like any other boy. It was small gestures like these that made me feel as though my life were finally normalizing. I was a mom, and he was my son. We were a normal family.

It was easy to pass the time as we spoke with another friend that was there with her son. Kris' son, Kyler, had been admitted within a day or two of Ty's birth to wait for a heart transplant. In June, he had finally received his heart and was on the rocky road to recovery. Kris had come down to our room and we caught up on other kids in the PICU we had left behind on June 8. Kris joked with me over Ty's unkempt fingernails. I explained to her that I had tried once to cut them and had gone too short on one and made him cry. That was the first and last time I attempted cutting them. She laughed as she said, "The trick is to do it while they sleep, silly." She found a pair of small scissors and trimmed them for me, teasing me the whole time that I could handle everything else but couldn't cut his nails. I can't explain why, but this small act still stands out in my mind. I can still see Kris with those little scissors, cutting Ty's nails so lovingly. She was a great friend, and I was so thankful we had met her.

Finally, after what seemed like forever, they were ready to do the cath. Dr. Hirsch came in and went over all of the risks with us, and discussed what he planned to do and what he expected to find. It had long been suspected that Ty was now receiving too much blood flow to his lungs since the second shunt was put in, and this cath would confirm or rule out those suspicions. Depending on what they found, Ty's surgery could be anywhere from a month to several months away.

As we signed the authorization forms and listened to the list of complications possible with such a procedure, I remember telling Dr. Hirsch, "I trust you. I know you'll take good care of him." --and that was no bluff-I did trust him completely.

We waited less time than we had expected to, and took the quick return of Dr. Hirsch as a sign that all was well. When he came in to explain what he had found, however, we got other news. His lungs were receiving way too much blood. One lung in particular was in danger of being permanently compromised if this continued, and surgery would need to be sooner rather than later . . . as soon as next week to be exact. My heart raced, my face felt hot and red and I struggled to understand. When Dr. Hirsch exited the room, I began to cry. I remember rising to my feet and crying, asking "Why? It wasn't enough that he's got a bad heart and is mentally handicapped, and *now* he may not be able to breathe, either?" Thoughts raced through my mind at a million miles per hour. I would have to bring him into this hospital again next week? It would not be like it was on our last weekend visit. This time, they would open his chest again. They would open his tiny little chest and hold his heart in their hands again. Where was my miracle? As if it were not enough that he would once again have to endure a life-threatening surgery, I would have to once again surrender my mothering to the nurses. Don't get me wrong, I loved the PICU nurses, and trusted them completely. But, in the PICU, parents are not allowed to sleep in the room. Would I have to go home at night, without my son, and leave him until morning with nurses to take my place? How was I to sleep without him next to my head in his boppy pillow? He and I slept inches from one another. I knew that every night he was right there. I could hear him breathe. I could smell him, fresh from his bath, right there next to me. At times, I would even put my head on the corner of his little pillow so that I could feel him next to my skin. How was I expected to go home without him for up to several weeks as he recovered? And what would be the outcome of this surgery? Would his lungs be okay? Would he be on a ventilator? What was going to happen?

Where was my miracle????

*Chapter 28*

# RELIEF BY THE NAME OF AMY

THOSE FEARS SOMEWHAT SUBSIDED AS they brought Ty back to his room. His tiny little body was lying sedated in that bed, a tube down his throat and a ventilator at his side . . . next week did not matter anymore.

I sat by his side and talked to him. He had been given a paralytic as well as anesthesia to keep him from making even the slightest movement as they put a catheter the size of a hair through his groin and into his heart . . . even the smallest twitch could be fatal. As he slowly came in and out of consciousness, he was obviously frustrated by his inability to move due to the paralytic. Such a horrifying sight, seeing my beautiful boy lie there completely motionless, like a baby doll. I knew he was awake inside of that paralyzed body, and it broke my heart.

Until he became fully alert, he would not be taken off of the ventilator. Once extubated, he would need to wait a few hours before he ate to be sure he did not need to be re-intubated, something they could not do with food in his stomach. What did all this mean? It meant that he still would not be fed for several more hours, and he was hungry NOW!

Travis sat by his side and whispered things I could not hear as I spoke to the charge nurse. The shift was changing, and I wanted to find out if we could get one of our "primary nurses" to take care of him that night. During our first 6 weeks there, we had several nurses over and over again, and compiled a "primary nurse" list. This meant that if any of them were on duty, they would likely be assigned to care for Ty. This was nice because it avoided reacquainting each new nurse with his condition, and also made us feel more confident in leaving him at night. We knew his primary nurses well, and knew that they loved him as their own child. The charge nurse checked her list, and saw that one our favorite nurses, Amy, would be on duty. She promised that we would get Amy that night, and I was relieved.

When Amy came in, she was excited to see "our little man" as she called him. She loved Ty so much. I had even brought her a picture at her request that day, hoping that she would be there to receive it. She kept a photo album at home of all of her "kids", and had asked me last time to bring her a photo. We talked for a while, and I felt so relieved that she was there. Ty was awakening more quickly than the doctors had expected. If he kept doing as well as he was, he would be extubated and eating soon.

Eventually, the doctor on duty that night came in to evaluate him. She said she felt he was ready to be extubated, and discussed with Amy what meds he should be given. Ty had a list of several meds he received twice a day, but he had not gotten them yet because he needed to have an empty stomach for the procedure. I remember her telling Amy not to give him his Digoxin, a prescription that helped his heart pump more efficiently. I asked her, "You mean you can do that?" We had been so religious with delivering his meds at the exact same time each day, and she was going to let him skip a dose? She answered me with a smile and said, "Well, *I* can, but you can't at home."

I was so proud of my little man as he began to wake up. Travis laughed at my disbelief in his quick recovery. He explained that he had been having a talk with Ty when I was away, and told him he needed to wake up so we could get home in time for Mommy's birthday. It was as though he listened, because nearly immediately after that conversation, he began to rustle around and fight the tube in his throat—he wanted it out.

He was extubated with no problems and was groggy but awake. He was now fully aware of just how long it had been since he had eaten. It was probably 1:00 am by now, and he was not happy about it. I held him and rocked him, snuggling him against my chest. I whispered to him, "Just a little longer, buddy. Go to sleep for a while and when you wake up, you'll get to eat." Eventually, he went to sleep, and I was relieved. He had had a rough day, and it broke my heart to deny him the food that he so longed for. I begged and pleaded with the doctor to feed him, but she asked that we wait another hour or two.

With Ty finally asleep, I laid him in the hospital bed and Travis and I decided to try to take a nap ourselves. We wanted to be wide awake when it was time to feed him, but were exhausted from a long day of worry. We could have slept in the parents' lounge, but Travis suggested going to the parking lot and catching a quick nap in the truck. Amy assured me that she would be with Ty and I asked her to call me if he should wake up and be fussy again. I trusted Amy as though she were family, and knew that Ty was in good hands. She double checked the cell phone number she had, and we exited those automatic double doors for what seemed like the one millionth time in Ty's life.

What God knew at this moment, and what I was about to learn, was that it was nearly time to say goodbye for good this time. My world was about to be shattered, all of my dreams crushed. I exited that PICU a confident mother for the very last time, there in those early morning hours. I had just rocked my boy to sleep for the very last time. I lay him to rest in that enormous, stark bed, thinking I would soon return to take him home and celebrate my first birthday as a mother.

If only I had known that was the last time I would ever feel his breath on my face. If I had only known that I would never again open my eyes in the morning and have his beautiful face there to greet me, just inches away. If I had only known that I would never brush his perfect hair or kiss his sweet little lips . . . I would have never left his side.

That's the beauty of God's omniscience. He knew that I would never have left Ty there if I thought there was a problem. He had had a plan all along, and my leaving the PICU was part of it. Ty's time here was over, the pain was gone, and I had truly been touched by an angel.

I didn't see his wings the day he was born. I was too busy seeing his tell-tale eyes, his low ears, and that roll on the back of his neck that told me he was not the 'perfect' son I had planned on. No, I didn't look hard enough to see those wings, because I didn't want to. I was so busy watching for God's hand to reach down and heal him that I missed the wings tucked neatly behind his tiny body. They were waiting there for the day I could let go.

Surely they were aching to open up and fly him away from here. Kindly, though, he waited for me to leave that glass room full of beeps and fear – and then he revealed them. He protected me from those wings, kept them out of sight as not to scare me or hurt me any more than his illness already had.

We had been in the truck just long enough to lay the seats back and close our eyes when the cell phone rang. Travis answered, and said "Okay, we'll be right in." My heart sank and I dove up. "What?" I asked. He assured me that it was the nurse's desk, and all she said was that she needed us to come back in.

As I ran across the street and into the doors of the hospital, I knew in my heart something was terribly wrong. It was as though everything was in slow motion, almost like running through deep water. Inside I was running with all of my might toward those elevators, but it felt like a cartoon in which all time had been dramatically slowed.

I *had* to get to my boy. I *had* to get to that floor. I *had* to get to those doors; the dreaded double doors of fear that had tormented me nearly every day for three months. Suddenly, the horrid hospital scents that lingered in the air vanished. Beeps of pumps and alarms on monitors fell silent as I ran in slow motion through the nightmare that was unfolding. I felt a sense of urgency that compelled me to the PICU, completely clueless of what waited for me beyond those damned double doors.

Little did I know that I would soon stand in that PICU for the last time. Hovering out of my body, in a place of slowed time, I would glare at the flashing 'code' light above the door of the room. I would watch the hustle and bustle of nurses and doctors, just as I had seen so many times before. It was nothing new, really; lights flashing, nurses sweating, crash carts rolling down the hall. This time, though, they would be changing MY life. This time, they would look ME in the eye with solemn faces, and deliver the same news they had undoubtedly delivered hundreds of times before.

We were still standing in the same spot, there in the hallway of the PICU, having given permission to discontinue resuscitation efforts, when Dr. Hirsch came in. He had been called from his bed I'm sure by his appearance. He looked at me in disbelief and asked, very simply, "What happened?" He could not explain it, and did not know what to say. He hugged me, said how sorry he was, and went in to see what he could find out. I was hoping he would have an explanation, but he was as shocked as we were.

We were finally allowed into his room. There he lay, and he looked so tiny there, bundled in a blanket. It had been so long since I had looked at him so objectively. He looked like a tiny speck there in that big bed. He was already cold, and he looked different. Through tears, I spoke words that seemed to flow from me as though I had rehearsed them. I kissed him over and over, and told him to tell God thank you for giving him to me, and to tell Jesus thank you, too. I was in shock, and yet at peace. I did not hold him. I did not need to. Ty was not in that bed, he was gone. I did not want to hold the shell he had inhabited . . . I knew he was in the room, but that was not him anymore.

Travis said his goodbyes, and word traveled quickly through the 7th floor. Several nurses came in to pay their respects and we finally got to hear what happened. Amy explained it all:

She had been outside of his door when the alarm started sounding. She assumed that one of the EKG leads had come loose, because she had just been in his room. She went in to check on him, and silenced the alarm. As she checked the leads, she called to him but he did not respond. She looked at the monitor and saw that his heart rate was plummeting. She tried to awaken him, but could not. She called for help, and began to attempt to resuscitate him. She could not explain what happened, but assured me that she had never left his side. She cried with me as she told me how much she loved him, and us. We were like family, in a way . . . and I knew she was genuine when she hugged me.

We had been out of his room only minutes. We probably were not even to the truck when he died. In fact, it happened so quickly, Amy actually sent someone to the elevator to look for us, because she thought surely we would still be that close.

I know that he waited for us to leave before he went. He did not want me to live with knowing he died in my arms, and he knew we did not need to witness him leaving us.

The staff followed protocol, asking if we wanted our church notified. We requested that they call our priest, as Ty had not ever been baptized. We wound up having to use a hospital pastor to baptize him, something we had been planning to do at church surrounded by family and friends. I even had the letters all typed and ready for the aunt and uncle we planned to ask to be his Godparents. Once again, things had spun terribly out of control. This was not how I had expected it to go.

We talked a while, and I rubbed the hair I loved so much for the last time. I told him how proud I was of him, that I loved him with all of my heart, and that I was so thankful that he was mine. He was mine, and now he was gone.

I found peace in knowing that he was surrounded by Amy's love in those last moments. She assured me that he had never awakened after I laid him in the bed. He went peacefully in his sleep, and I was thankful.

We were taken across the hall to make the phone calls we never thought we'd make. We struggled to remember telephone numbers, completely unaware of what time it even was. One by one, we woke our loved ones to give them the news.

Many of Ty's primary nurses came in to talk to us. It was nice to see how much they loved him, and I was sure to tell each of them how much we loved and appreciated them and all they had done for us.

Travis went back into Ty's room to gather his things. We were suddenly leaving the hospital alone again. This time we pushed his stroller, filled with his favorite things, and he was not with us. Passing through those PICU doors, something we had done a million times before, so many things went through my head. I thought of the day that lay ahead, my birthday, a day that I thought would be filled with triumph after the wonderful results Ty would have from his cath. I still could not understand what had happened, why it happened, how God could *let* it happen. My mind wandered to strange things, like how his little nails had just been trimmed. The words of all the people we had seen that day swarmed through my head like a tornado; one I could not keep up with. I kept picturing him lying in that big bed, looking so handsome with his newly blonde hair and beautiful blue eyes. I remembered how our nurse had said she was trying not to treat us like patients, since we were just there for some tests. <u>No</u> <u>one</u> had seen this coming! We were only there for tests, routine procedures . . . why were we leaving alone?

We had left some of Ty's belongings downstairs at the nurses' desk, the most important of which was his beloved mobile. He adored that thing, with its brightly colored animals and classical music. As I walked away from the desk with his mobile in my hand, I thought of how much he loved it, and couldn't believe I was taking it home never to be watched again.

It was then that I saw a family sitting in the waiting area. Once again, I spoke as though from out of my own body, and tearfully said, "I don't know why you are here today, but be thankful for what you have." I didn't turn around to see their reaction, I just kept walking.

As we exited the hospital, we both looked into the sky. I know that Ty was there, and the dawn sky was the most amazing, vibrant blue either of us had ever seen. Travis could not help but laugh, and said "That's my boy. He knows Daddy's favorite color is blue." It was beautiful. More beautiful than any painting had ever depicted, any poet had ever written. I know that Ty was there, and I know that was his way of saying he was okay. I'll never forget the way that sky looked. I can see it anytime I want, just by closing my eyes.

*Chapter 29*

# ALONE AGAIN

W E WENT HOME, ALONE. THE ride home was a blur, and I thank God we got there safely because we were in no shape to drive. Much like the day we received the news of his heart-defects, we were once again let loose into the world, completely unprepared. I cannot even remember if we spoke the whole hour home. We were in such a state of disbelief. We had not planned for this. We had experienced so many things that week that we considered signs of good things to come . . . how could this be happening?

We walked in the door, and Travis began to work diligently, removing any sign of Ty in the house. I just seemed to float around in an alter-universe that was my home . . . an empty home that soon showed no sign of my beautiful boy's inhabitance. What had taken a year to collect, and two months to break in was gone. All signs of my sweet boy were gone in five minutes as Travis tore through the house. His beloved swing, which had been in front of the fireplace for 2 months, was quickly whisked away. His door was closed, and it was over. My life felt as though it had ended that morning. What was I to live for now? Everything I had dreamed of, everything I had lived for was gone. My heart felt so heavy and empty, my body was not my own; it was filled with so much grief that I did not have enough room for it all.

By this time it was probably 6 am. We tried to sleep, but as word spread, the phone rang off the hook. I didn't want to sleep, but I didn't want to be awake. I didn't really want to be alive. How could I outlive my son?

## Chapter 30

# JESUS' PHONE NUMBER

AFTER GETTING SOME SLEEP, WE got up and tried to figure out what to do with ourselves. It did not take long to realize that Ty was still there, even if I could not see him. I guess the first thing he did for us came that afternoon. I had been upset because of something as silly as a song I had stuck in my head. The verse, 'Jeremiah was a Bullfrog' ran over and over in my mind. "How could I be thinking of a stupid song at a time like this?" Disgusted with myself, I finally said something to Travis. He looked at me and laughed. "You've got to be kidding," he said. "I've been thinking of that song, too." How could that be? It was odd enough that a song I never hear, and really don't even like was playing like a broken record in my mind. Now Travis was doing it, too? I blew it off and tried to keep busy.

That evening, Travis's parents came over to check on us. They didn't stay long, but as they left, his mother said something that nearly brought me to my knees. With one foot in the car, she looked over the roof of the car and said "You know Jesus' phone number, don't you?" We looked at her like she was crazy, and asked "What do you mean?" She replied, "Well, I've always heard that Jesus' phone number is Jeremiah 33:3. Look it up, you'll understand." I nearly died. Did she just say Jeremiah? We told her what we had been experiencing all day, and she proceeded to tell us what Jeremiah 33:3 was. It then made sense.

> *JEREMIAH 33:3*
> *CALL TO ME AND I WILL ANSWER YOU;*
> *I WILL TELL YOU THINGS GREAT BEYOND REACH OF YOUR KNOWLEDGE.*

Once again, I felt peace. I knew Ty was there with us. I knew that this was not coincidence. I believed it then, and I believe to this day . . . that was the first of many times that Ty would send us a message.

*Chapter 31*

# THE TRUE MIRACLES BEGAN

L ET IT BE KNOWN NOW that if you began reading this book with no faith, I hope you will end it believing. If you have faith, it will be renewed and strengthened. The things I will tell you in the chapters to follow are true. I have experienced things that I know with every ounce of my being are miracles, ways that my son has reached me from Heaven. The intention behind writing this book was to share with you my experiences, and pray that they will touch you and open or re-open your heart. Some of these stories could be passed off by non-believers as coincidence. It's funny, isn't it? People believe they can make anything sound like coincidence if they try hard enough . . . yet if they would not try at all, they would see that miracles happen every day—one must just be open enough to see them for what they are.

## The Funeral

Here we were, preparing ourselves for a day we never thought would come . . . our son's funeral. The days approaching it were a confusing haze of sleepiness, exhaustion and pain. One thing was clear to me, though . . . I had to speak at the funeral. It was as though something just entered my body and consumed me. I HAD to tell everyone about my son. I had so many things to say, people to thank, and stories to tell. Things would pop into my head so frequently, I actually made a list of things that I needed to say. As you may expect, I was unable to sleep the night before. I couldn't sleep because so much was going through my mind, so many words I needed to say. They bombarded me . . . It was as though Ty was driving me to speak, and filling my mind and heart with the right words.

The morning of the funeral, I actually felt relief. I was anxious to get to the church, anxious to speak the words that ran through my head. I can still remember standing at the front, near his casket, and greeting everyone as they arrived. We had a display of pictures at the front, and blue and white balloons throughout the church. Everyone smiled and cried as they looked at that beautiful face that seemed to beam right off of the photos. It was strange, but I realized that morning that as we all hugged and cried, we had all been brought so much closer by Ty's life, and death. It was so comforting to watch our large family stream in, and it felt so good to see them smile as they looked at Ty's picture. In our hearts, we all knew he was in a better place. We were sad for ourselves, and happy for him.

When the time came for me to speak, I was ready. With my Bible and notes in hand, I approached the microphone. I looked out at the sea of familiar faces, and began to speak. Words came out of me as though I was not even the one speaking. I did not get hysterical, but simple, love-filled tears fell down my cheeks as I celebrated my son. As I looked at the blue and white balloons that floated before me, I knew that this was indeed a celebration of Ty's life. I urged everyone not to feel sad that day, but yet to be happy and join me in celebrating my beautiful son. I told the story of Jeremiah 33:3, and watched the faces of my loved ones as they listened. I saw tears stream down faces of even the strongest men, and I knew then the love that Ty had brought with him. I had so many things to say. I encouraged the expectant parents not to live in fear of "what might happen," but yet to know that God had chosen them to be parents to that unborn child, and to trust that things would be okay. I thanked everyone for the love they showed the three of us during our hardest times, and assured them that Ty was aware of how much they loved him.

I spoke of Ty's beauty, and the sparkling blue eyes that seemed to captivate everyone he met. As I described them, I could see everyone nodding their heads. They could picture those clear blue eyes just as I could . . . and we all knew that those eyes were embodied by someone special. Everyone had noticed Ty's eyes, and I knew that they would live on in everyone's memory.

I could not leave without reading to them a newspaper article that was published the week Ty was born. It had been given to me by two different sisters-in-law, neither knowing that the other had seen it. It was entitled "Jesus Lives in Human Hearts," by Catherine Gallasso. As I reflected on my son's life during the days leading up to the funeral, I came across the article that had been given to me 3 months earlier. As I re-read it, I realized that I had been *meant* to read it. I have no doubt that God made sure that article was given to me. The article told the story of a 6 year old boy awaiting heart surgery. I will share with you an excerpt, as you cannot fully appreciate the impact of this article without reading it yourselves:

*"In the examining room, the parents and their 6-year-old son sat quietly as the surgeon spoke. 'In the morning, I will open your son's heart,' he said. With a light shining in his eyes, the little boy interrupted. 'You'll find Jesus there.'*

*The surgeon looked up in shock. Then he continued, 'I will see how much damage has been done.'*

*Again, the boy said, 'You'll find Jesus there. He lives in my heart.'*

*With a slight frown, the surgeon stated to the parents, 'I'm sure there are weakened vessels, low blood supply and damaged muscles. When I operate, we will hope for the best.'*

*With that, he left the room and went back to his office. Sitting down at his desk, he looked again at the little boy's records and x-rays.*

*'Why,' asked the surgeon, 'Why do these things happen?' Turning to God for the first time in his life, he asked, 'Why have you brought*

*this little boy here for such a short time? You made him. You created his weak heart. Why?'*

*Then, to his great surprise, the surgeon felt the awesome presence of God speak deep within his own heart.*

*'The boy belongs to me. He is my lamb and his purpose on earth is accomplished. He has retrieved for me another lamb. He will come back into my arms and his parents will follow later.'*

*Such a great revelation of God's love enveloped the surgeon that he put his head down on his desk and wept.*

*After surgery, the worried parents sat with the surgeon by the boy's hospital bed.*

*When the lad awoke, he looked at the surgeon wearily and asked, 'Did you cut open my heart?'*

*The surgeon replied, 'Yes, son.'*

*'What did you find?' whispered the boy.*

*With joy and tears in his eyes, the surgeon said, 'I found Jesus there, and He found me.'*

*If you seek God with all your heart, you will surely find Him."*


As I read this article, staring through teary eyes at my loved ones, I could see the light come on in their eyes, and in their hearts. It was as though they realized, then, some for the first time, that Ty had a purpose. He had completed his mission here, and we would all be together again someday. It warmed my heart to see them look back at me as I stood at that microphone—I knew that Ty had done his job, and he had done it well. I looked at all those people there to honor him, and knew that he had touched each one of them in a different way.

Some of them had re-opened their hearts to God. Some of them realized that things don't always go as we plan. Some of them had a new outlook on their lives, and realized that maybe *their* lives weren't as hard as they had once thought. No matter what the message was, one thing was shared by each person there, they had each been touched by <u>my</u> son. I was so proud of him at that moment.

It's funny, but we sat in the front pew, right next to Ty's casket. Even though I was that close to his body, I knew that he was not there. It did not bother me to be so close, because I knew that he was even closer – he was sitting beside me, holding my hand.

With his casket was his faithful companion, the silver angel his daddy bought him before he was born. Around the angel's neck was Ty's rosary. It was given to him by friends of the family, and they had had it blessed for him. That silver angel, along with that rosary, had accompanied Ty to every hospital trip. It was in his hospital bed, and went with him to surgery. The angel had gone everywhere with him, and this final trip would be no exception. It was buried with him, too. I can still see that angel, kneeling gently in Ty's bed, a colorful rosary around his neck. Sometimes I miss it, and wish that I could hold it close. It is where it needs to be though, with Ty's physical body, where it had been since he was born.

After the funeral, everyone commented on the words I had spoken. They were all touched, and were shocked at my ability to stay calm and speak. I tried to explain to them that I was compelled to speak, Ty wanted me to speak, and he spoke through me that day. I spoke to one friend, a Board member at the ambulance district that I had known for years. As he hugged me, I told him I was sorry he had never had the privilege of meeting Ty. He looked at me, smiled and said, "After hearing you talk about him, I feel like I have met him. I can almost see those blue eyes."

I knew then I had done my job; I had done Ty justice.

## Life Goes On

The days after the funeral were a little easier than the days leading up to it. I finally got to say all I had to say, and I knew that we had made some kind of closure.

As I thought of Ty, which was nearly every second, many things took on a new light, and I made many new realizations. My mind began to reel, much like the fast forward button had been pressed. Just like the moment when a movie plot begins to come together, and bits and pieces of previous scenes flash across the screen and BOOM! It all makes sense!

I began to think about the healing mass we had attended that week. I thought about what the priest had asked, when he thought Ty had a lung problem. As it turned out, we did find out during the cardiac cath that he *was* having trouble with his lungs, they were being flooded with blood. *Did the priest know that?* What about that day in his swing? Was he indeed looking at something? Perhaps the angels had come to visit him and prepare him for coming home with them. Who really know what happens before we die?

As I struggled through the days, I would find myself in his room, smelling his things. I held his Boppy pillow close, and sucked every last bit of his scent from it. I looked at his beautiful bed, waiting patiently to have someone placed inside of it. I had wanted that bed so badly, and Ty had never even used it. I held his clothes close to my heart, and patted them as though I were patting his back to calm him. I reflected on the last time I held him, and on how I had calmed him back to sleep. I missed him so much, and longed to feel him in my arms. It is hard for me even now to reflect on those feelings, and I write this with tears streaming down my cheeks as I long to hold my precious boy again.

No one can prepare you for the love you feel for your children, your flesh and blood. More so than that, no one can prepare you for the pain of losing a child. My prayer for each of you as you read this is that you never experience what I have. For those of you that have lost a child, I hope that you find peace in reading Ty's story, and know that your child is with you through everything that you do. You will hold your child close again, someday, just as I will. We will again smell their sweet scent, stroke their hair and feel their soft skin. It will feel as though we were never apart, and as for me, I cannot wait.

## Butterflies

It had been just a few days, and I had spent the majority of them talking to Ty. As I sat on the porch swing watching Travis cut the grass, I had a long conversation with Ty. Travis had looked over at me and just smiled . . . he saw me talking, and knew that I was talking to my little monkey again.

"Can you give me a sign?" I asked. "Just a little something to let me know you're here, and you're okay. Ask God if it's okay for you to send me a little sign." I wasn't sure what to expect, but I longed for a little something from my precious boy. I waited for a cool breeze, a twinkle in the sky, something . . .

Just then, a beautiful butterfly flew under the awning of the porch, around the swing I sat on, and back out across the lawn. My heart raced as I asked Ty, "Was that you?" I paused for a minute, basking in what had just happened. "You know, I *think* that was you, but you know I am a little hard headed and sometimes you have to be very obvious for Mommy. If that was you, can you give me another, more obvious sign?" I felt bad, as though I was really making him work hard, but I couldn't help myself. I sat and held my breath, waiting. Then, it happened. A huge shadow was cast over our entire yard. As I looked at the houses surrounding ours, I saw nothing but beautiful sunshine beaming across their grass. It was obvious that the shadow was only over OUR yard, and I knew then that that was my sign. After about a minute, the shadow disappeared. My heart raced, and I thanked Ty; he had given me my sign.

It was then that I knew that Ty had sent me that butterfly. Was that him? Had he taken on the form of a butterfly now? I was not sure . . . yet. But it did not take long for me to get my answer.

## Gone, but not forgotten

It was clear to see that though Ty was not physically here, he was not actually gone at all. Everyone thought of Ty often, and even his cousins spoke of him. As small children, I figured that they would quickly forget Ty. Quite to the contrary, some of the smallest kids gave me the biggest surprises. Several of his aunts actually told me that the kids were praying for Ty every night, and would talk to him and ask him questions. "Hey, Baby Ty," his 3-year-old cousin Brendan said, "What you doing up there in those clouds? You playing up there with Jesus?" His 6-year-old cousin Sami had looked up at the sky with her mom, and had explained that she knew Ty was up there sitting on one of those clouds watching her. It was as though he had reached even the smallest of hearts, and had left a mark that would never be erased. To this day they remember him, and love him . . . and that makes me so happy.

## More Butterflies

It didn't take long for the butterflies to visit me again. Travis and I had been debating on buying a piece of property we had stumbled across. It was 11 1/2 acres, and we could just see our little house sitting in the middle of that green grass. We had been weighing our options for a while, and on the afternoon of August 25, I decided to drive out and spend some time there with Ty.

As I looked out over the overgrown grass and weeds that lay before me, I had a talk with Ty. "Is this where Mommy and Daddy should be?" I asked. "Should your little brothers and sisters run and play in this yard someday?"

I was saddened when no obvious sign smacked me in the head to tell me "YES, buy it!" I waited around a while, waiting for something to happen. I'm sure I looked quite pathetic standing around twiddling my thumbs waiting for the wind to blow or the earth to shake . . . just waiting for that sign. Finally, I decided that maybe we were not meant to buy the land, and figured I should head home. As I got into the truck and began to drive away, I looked to my left. It was then that I had to slam on the brakes in disbelief. Filling the ditch along the roadside were dozens of butterflies. As I drove along, they kept up the pace and stayed right along side of me. It was as though they were just following me, waiting for me to notice them. I stopped, backed up, and got out of the truck again. I was overwhelmed with emotion, seeing this swarm of tiny creatures buzzing right along with me. I took that as my sign that Ty wanted us to buy that property. He was probably laughing his head off at my impatience as I started to leave. If I had to guess, I would say he just wanted me to have to wait for a minute before he gave me my answer. My heart raced, just as it had that day on the porch swing, as I looked at the swarm of butterflies delivering my son's message to me.

**It was confirmed, my son was now a butterfly.**

## Ty's Last Job . . . and More Butterflies!

Just three days later, on August 28, 2001, I learned of Ty's last job on earth. I had been lonely at home all day, Travis had gone back to work, and I had just a few weeks before resigning from the job I loved so much. I missed the coworkers who had become my friends long before, and then had become my family throughout my ordeal with Ty. They were there for me during my pregnancy, and I missed them all so much. I felt so out of place being at home. I had essentially grown up with my coworkers, having started there at only 18, I had spent the past 6 years with that small group that I now missed so much.

I had decided to spend some time at an antique store, trying to pass the minutes and hours until Travis came home that evening. My cell phone rang, and it was Travis. He had a question for me or something, and I happened to mention to him that I had not been feeling well that morning. He laughed hysterically and said, "Well, maybe you're pregnant." I quickly corrected him, telling him that would not be funny at all and he should not even joke about such things.

I went on about my day, but could not totally put behind me what he had said. "Could I be pregnant?" I don't see how it could be possible, but now the question weighed on my mind.

I went home, and tried to talk myself out of taking a pregnancy test. As hard as I tried, I knew that there was one pregnancy test left in the closet from the ones I had bought with Ty . . . and I finally gave in and took it.

As I looked down at the single line, I felt relieved and threw the test away. An hour or so later, I happened to be in the bathroom again and for some reason decided to take one more look at that test. This time, I thought I saw a very faint second line. Just as I had done almost exactly one year before, I got butterflies in my stomach. I couldn't decide if I was happy, sad or crazy . . . but I began to feel sick and ran to the truck. I had to get more tests, NOW.

I talked to Ty all the way to the store. I told him that I knew he already knew the answer to my question, and that I was sure he was laughing at me, but I could not help myself. I explained to him that this was exactly what I had done when I found out I was pregnant with him. Once again I was in the same truck going to the same store to get pregnancy tests. I told him he could just hush up because I was sure he was just busting a gut laughing at his idiot mother as she sped to the store. I could just see him laughing at me, but I didn't care . . . . I had to know.

The second test was the same as the first; one very obvious line, and a very, very, very faint second line.

I waited for Travis to come home, just as I had done a year before. He arrived to another package, wrapped in shiny paper with a ribbon. This time, though, he knew what that package meant before he even opened it. "I'm not 100% sure," I explained. It didn't matter, though, he was thrilled. I, however, was in shock.

I waited a few days, then took the third test. This time, that second line showed up just as obvious as the first. I was pregnant . . . Oh crap, I was pregnant!

In shock and disbelief, I made a doctor's appointment for September 8, just to be sure. I didn't know how it was humanly possible for me to be pregnant. September 8 was a Saturday, and we happened to have tickets to a Cardinals baseball game. My brother Marty, 14 at the time, was coming along. I wasn't sure how I'd explain the stop at the doctor's office, but he didn't ask many questions, so I didn't give many answers. Travis and I went in to see the doctor while Marty waited outside. We explained all that had happened in the past few months, and Dr. Lange (a new doctor for me) listened caringly to our story. It was then time for the news we were waiting so desperately to receive . . . . and it was confirmed. I was indeed pregnant, we were indeed going to have another baby, and I was indeed about to fall off of that table when he gave me the next bit of information----------

My estimated due date? May 5, 2002. Why was this the icing on the cake, you ask? Well, you see, Ty's due date was May 5, 2001. It was miraculous enough that I was pregnant, but to have the same due date was just unheard of. I took this as my sign that this baby was indeed a miracle, and tried to regain my composure as we entered the waiting room where Marty sat patiently.

I tried to stay cool, and not let the cat out of the bag. We went on to our baseball game, and arrived just a few minutes after it had started. We were having a wonderful day; the weather was beautiful, a little hot, but absolutely beautiful. The game was great, and during the 7$^{th}$ inning stretch, Ty stopped in to say "Hello."

It wasn't until Marty elbowed me that I began to see what he had spotted. "Hey, Jenn, is that a butterfly out there?" I peered out across the field, and as sure as there was sun in the sky there was a butterfly flying around the field. I cannot logically explain how we could see this butterfly from our seats, or how Marty spotted it . . . but there it was. I elbowed him back and said "See, Ty just wanted to tag along today." It was just a few minutes later that I was pushed straight over the emotional edge when the big television screens began to show images of kids with Down Syndrome in an ad for the Buddy Walk. It was all a little too much for one day, I guess, but they were tears of joy and love that streamed down my face . . . right there in the middle of a packed stadium. I tried to hold them back, but it was too much. I probably looked like a moron, but I didn't care. I was going to have a baby, and Ty was right there by my side. What more could I ask for?

# Chapter 32

# SPILLING THE BEANS

I T WAS ALL SO OVERWHELMING, the news that we had received that day.
I wasn't able to keep it a secret like I did the first time, and we spilled
the beans to my mom, my brother, Marty and Travis's parents that night.
They were all so excited, and so were we. Scared, but excited. I knew that
this child was definitely a miracle, and hoped and prayed that things would
be different this time.

This pregnancy was so different from the first. I was sick as a dog,
finding myself thankful to not be working, because I could do nothing
but lie on the couch until late afternoon. Just a simple trip to the bathroom
made me feel wretched, and I hoped that this was a sign that this pregnancy
would go better.

On November 20, we had our first ultrasound. Well, we had had one
before, just to check the due date, but this was the first *real* ultrasound. My
doctor had wanted me to be comfortable with this pregnancy, and knew
how scared I was, so he sent me to a large hospital with more advanced
equipment. I had been there before, with Ty. My stomach ached as we went
in, and I felt as though an elephant sat on my chest as we waited for what
seemed like an eternity in the waiting room. Once inside, the wait was just
as bad. This was a busy place, and appointments never went as scheduled.
We waited in that room for a while, and I lay there on the table with knots

in my stomach. When the doctor finally came in, I wasn't sure if I was ready for this or not. We talked briefly about Ty, discussed the likelihood of reoccurrence, then began the ultrasound. When we looked at the heart, I could see that it was different from Ty's. I didn't know what I was looking at with Ty, I hadn't ever seen a heart before. But, now, looking at this one, I could see that it was very different. My whole body got hot, and I could feel my face getting red. I wasn't sure if *different* was good or bad, and the silence seemed to cut through my body as I waited for a response.

It was music to my ears, as she said "Everything looks good." I couldn't believe it. The heart, the fluid, the abdomen, everything . . . everything looked great. I was overjoyed as tears streamed down my face and I thanked her for the best news of my life . . . I was going to have a healthy baby!

The walk to the car was so much easier that day. I had been so afraid to have an ultrasound just before Christmas again, since last year had been so terrible. I thought about the numbness we had felt last year, walking to the car in the ice and snow, our minds echoing the words of the doctors from just minutes before. This time was different, though. We were overjoyed, and our walk to the car was triumphant. We were going to have a healthy baby. God had given us a healthy baby. Who needs gifts? We had everything we could ask for for Christmas.

## Chapter 33

# IMPATIENTLY WAITING

I FOUND MYSELF IN A different position during this pregnancy. With Ty, I didn't want to give birth. I wanted to keep him inside of me forever, because there he would be safe and healthy. I knew that as long as he was in me, and I was helping him live, he would be okay. I feared labor, and birth, and wished that my pregnancy would go on forever.

This time, though, I was so excited. I could not wait to meet my child, and it made the time go slower. It was as though I had spent years being pregnant, and I guess in a way I had. I had only had a brief 2 month break between pregnancies, so I had essentially been pregnant for nearly 2 years. I had grown accustomed to being huge, hungry and unable to sleep comfortably. I instinctively stopped and crossed my legs before coughing or sneezing (any mother will understand why), and I actually still do that out of habit. I was the eternally-pregnant woman, and I was ready for it to be over.

I did what I could to keep myself occupied at home. I had begun my own little craft projects which, with Travis's help, turned into enough to even do a couple of craft shows that spring. This kept me busy, and wound up doing a lot more as well.

It was our first craft show, and I was so excited. We had a lot of things made, including shelves, tables and cabinets. We set up our booth and the crowd began to flow in. It was mid-afternoon when a wonderful thing happened. I cannot do justice to its power with mere words, but I will try my best. To recall it brings a chill up my back and makes my heart beat just a little faster. As we sat side by side watching the crowd to pass the time, we noticed a woman walking by with her twin boys. About 3 years old, they were beautiful with their blonde hair and blue eyes; each holding their mother's hand as they whisked past the booths in a hurry. As they neared our booth, one of the boys was immediately drawn to Travis. We could feel his stare upon us as he approached, and suddenly we were thrust into a series of events that warmed our hearts and brought tears to our eyes. As the trio got closer, the boy's face lit up as he began to repeat "Hi, Daddy! Hi, Daddy!" Travis and I looked at each other, then back at the boy only to find that this warm welcome was directed at Travis. "Hi, Daddy, Hiiiiiii!" he said again as he neared us. His free little hand waved as fast as it could as he just beamed with elation . . . . . "Hi, Daddy, Hi!" he said again. He was calling Travis "Daddy". By this time, we were nearly face to face, and the boy was surely old enough to see that Travis was not his daddy. But, yet, he persisted his quest to greet his "Daddy" as he stood just feet in front of us. He was never discouraged by the look of disbelief and utter shock we must have displayed; he simply glowed with love and waved and talked to Travis until he was gone. I guess the strangest part of the entire episode was that the boy's mother and brother never seemed to acknowledge any of it. They stared straight ahead, as though never having heard his very loud conversation with his "Daddy." The boy stood within a few feet of us, staring Travis directly in the face and warmly repeated "Hi, Daddy!" over and over again, his sweet little hand waving as fast as it could. I cannot explain how this boy could mistake Travis for his father, nor can I understand how the mother of a toddler could not notice that her son was calling someone else Daddy. It was as though everyone else in the building had left, and it was only the three of us there. Everything disappeared, and we seemed to be in slow motion as this beautiful blonde-headed boy made my heart skip a beat. I have often wondered what Ty would've looked like at that age, and have always felt that that boy may have been sent there just to deliver a message to us. It was as though Ty were right there in front of us again, stopping by just to say "Hello, Daddy. I'm okay, don't worry."

*Chapter 34*

# IT'S TIME!

EASTER CAME AND WENT AND I was once again big as a house for the holiday. I tried to be spunky as my ankles swelled and my face got huge, but inside I was ready to go.

As one last retreat before chaos, Travis and I decided to make a trip to Florida. My doctor gave me the go-ahead to drive, as long as I took a break and walked every hour and a half. The car ride was long, especially making frequent pit stops, but we arrived in beautiful Florida safely. I had not traveled much, and was so excited to enjoy the warmth of the sun and the hot sand on my swollen feet. We had a great time, going where the wind took us. We made no lodging arrangements in advance, we just *went*. It was wonderful to feel so carefree, though in the back of my mind I kept wondering if my child would be a native Floridian . . . I was 8 ½ months pregnant after all, and could've had that baby right there on vacation.

All went well, though, and junior did not make a surprise guest appearance on our vacation. We met many nice people, and shared Ty's story several times along the way. It was wonderful.

Despite my excitement and pure elation about having a healthy child, my love for Ty and my desire to hold him in my arms did not fade. I thought of him often, and longed to hold him, touch him and smell him.

I knew that this baby would never replace him, but looked forward to once again holding my own flesh and blood in my arms. As it turned out, I wouldn't have to wait as long as I thought.

On the evening of April 22, 2002, Travis and I sat together on the couch watching TV. It was a typical evening, until I felt a swift kick unlike any I had ever felt. This baby overall had been far more active than Ty, but this kick was different. I barely had time to get a grunt out in response to it before I felt another strange feeling . . . .

"Oh my God, my water just broke!" I shouted out as I rolled off of the couch. Travis looked at me blankly and said, "Are you serious?" I think he thought I was pulling his leg until he looked down at mine. It was clear I wasn't joking around, and poor Travis ran through the house like a chicken with his head cut off grabbing towels. Bless his heart, there was no way I could move from my kneeling position for what seemed like his eternity, but he stood ready with his towel . . .

Once I finally made it into the bathroom, took a world record for speed shower, and got dressed, we headed to the hospital. There was no sense of urgency from my end, I hadn't yet begun to have contractions; but poor Travis felt enough urgency for both of us as he sped to the hospital with lightning speed. Having learned her lesson the first time, his mom opted to meet us at the hospital rather than risk her life riding along again! We got to the hospital safely, though, and I wiggled my way into admitting. I remember looking down at my belly in the parking lot and saying "Hey, my chest sticks out farther than my belly again!"

I never did have contractions on my own; I guess the baby changed its mind. They induced my labor with drugs, though, and my body kicked right. During the wait, we shared Ty's story with every nurse and doctor, and they were all so wonderful. They all looked at Ty's picture, commented on his beauty, and listened with loving ears.

My labor progressed quickly, and in just 7 short hours it was time to push. Though my doctor had not arrived yet, the baby was going to. I tried my hardest to hold it back, and in the nick of time, Dr. Lange came in the door. The baby came in only 2 pushes, and poor Dr. Lange was barely suited up. My heart pounded as I tried to see. I waited for that cry, and it seemed to take forever. Finally, I heard the cry, and Dr. Lange said "It's a girl!"

"I'm sorry . . . It's a WHAT?" I said. "A girl? How can it be a girl?" I had been convinced during my entire pregnancy that I was having a boy. I'm not sure why, since looking back the pregnancies were so opposite of each other, but regardless I was expecting a boy. I was so shocked that as the neonatal nurse cleaned the baby she jokingly said "Okay, now can I put the diaper on this baby or do you need to see one more time that it's a girl?"

I remember asking over and over, "Is she okay? Does she have Downs?" The caring nurse very calmly replied, "Well, let me see." She ever-so-lovingly looked at the baby; her hands, her neck, her ears . . . then simply replied "Well, she looks just fine to me!" I had never been so relieved. She was fine. She was missing a few parts I had expected her to have, but she was fine!

On April 23, 2002, just 6 days before Ty's 1st birthday,

Madysen Ty Naeger
weighed in at 6 lbs 1 ½ oz and 20 inches.

As I held her new body in my arms, and she looked up at me, I saw something so familiar; the same blue eyes I had seen just 359 days before. I know most babies are born with blue eyes, but these eyes were different. They had a sparkle, a depth about them that could not be described. They were Ty's eyes looking up at me through that tightly wrapped blanket. It was a special moment, and one I will never forget.

## Chapter 35

# A BABY IN THE HOUSE

IT WAS SO GREAT TO have another baby in the house. It was, however, hard to get used to a healthy baby. We were not accustomed to such low-maintenance. Mady ate from a bottle, slept lying flat and did not require medication.

I tried not to treat her like Ty, but I couldn't help it. I constantly stared at her color, lifted her shirt to check her breathing and stared at her all night. She slept in a bassinet 6 inches from my head for 3 months. I literally slept on my left side every night, all night so that all I had to do was open my eyes and I could see her. I was honestly afraid to roll over and turn my back to her, afraid that she may not be breathing when I awoke. It was a fear that consumed me at times, the fear that she was not as healthy as she appeared, that maybe there was something we had missed.

The fears finally lessened, and I eventually moved her into her room . . . into the beautiful round bed that had waited so long to hold a baby.

It was amazing to have her at home. It was uncomfortable at times, though. I actually missed having the monitors to rely on for accuracy. I didn't fully trust myself to be the sole judge of her health. I would've much preferred a monitor there to hook her up to occasionally for reassurance. Sick, in a way, but it was how I felt.

## Chapter 36

# SWEET BABY GIRL

MADY WAS AMAZING, AND ASIDE from not sleeping through the night, she was such an easy baby. She was very healthy, and very happy. She had a very unique personality from an early age, and was full of smiles and giggles. She was such a ham that I couldn't even go to the grocery store without people stopping me to play with her. I often described her as my little "nerd," because she just cracked me up all the time. I knew that Ty was a part of her, that those were his eyes and that I held a little piece of him every time I held her. It was so beautiful, and I was finally at peace.

She seemed to grow so fast, and she got smarter every day. She walked at 9 months, broke herself from a bottle at 11 months, and was a talker very early. She was the picture of health, and there was never a straight face in the room if she could help it. She was truly a clown from infancy. For that, I am so thankful.

I have been given a second chance at life, through Mady, I believe. I have been able to watch her grow, meet milestones and even exceed some of them. I have rocked her to sleep and felt her warm skin against mine. I saw her first toothless smile, heard her first laugh, and captured her first word on film, "Mama," she said, as she fought to climb onto my lap. The first time I trimmed her tiny little nails, I cried as I recalled Ty's first and last trim, recalling him once again lying in that big bed. It only takes a touch, a smell, a laugh, and I can go right back to that place. The place where all was good, and life was complete. The place where I heard my boy laugh for the first (and last) time. The place where Daddy's bright red shirt caught the eye of a sick little boy, and we were reminded that life was good. The place where I was first given the gift of amazing, unconditional love. I can go back there anytime I want, in my mind. For these gifts, I am truly thankful.

*Chapter 37*

# ROLL OVER, JESUS

A T TWO YEARS OLD, MADY knew her brother's pictures; she called him "Tite", but that's close enough for me. She knew Jesus, and could identify him in many forms, from crucifix to painting. She often talked about Jesus, and she knew his mother "Maerwy" and his father "Dofus". When she would see Jesus on the cross at church, she would call out to him "Hi, Jesus!" She blew him kisses and called out to him so loud that all the parishioners surely heard her. That's just Mady; she's an attention grabber.

Occasionally, she would go into more detail in her conversations with Jesus. She'd yell out "Hi, Jesus, up 'er on da cross. Roll over, Roll over!" She would wave her little hand with all her might and stand up on the kneeler to gain a little better view of her friend. I can't say *why* she asked him to "roll over ", but I think she wanted Him to get down from the cross and talk to her.

Honestly, I think He does. She always seemed to have an understanding of God, Jesus and her brother. It's a child-like understanding, but I know it's there. Sometimes she would call out to the air and wave "Hi, brother!" She recognized him in all pictures and occasionally referred to her own pictures as "Tite".

I don't really think that Mady is so different from any of us. We all want Jesus to "roll over" and get off of that cross. We long for Him to sit down on the couch with us, answer the "why's" in the world and give us all the answers. We all think that if He would just *speak* the world would be a better place. What's ironic is that when He does speak, so many of us don't listen.

You see, God talks to us every day. Okay, so you don't literally hear him say "Beverly, make a right turn at this stop sign." But, He's here, and unless we choose to listen, we will never hear what He has to say. He was there every time I prayed for Him to heal Ty's heart. He was there every time I cried, pleaded and begged for Him to take away Ty's pain and make it mine.

I am ashamed to say that though I always knew He was here, I didn't always choose to listen to Him before. Not until Ty entered my life did I truly open my eyes and my ears and say

### *"Okay, God. Talk to me. I'm ready to hear all you have to say."*

That's okay, though, because I know that He forgives me. I know because I continue to see Him in my life every day. I see Him answer my prayers, and I know that He has not forsaken me, even though I have at times forsaken Him. I ask Him every day to help me be a good person, to help others, and to live my life according to the plan He has for me. This book, I believe, is one way of doing that.

I did not choose to write this book. Not at first, anyway. I am no writer, and had not written since high school. It was not until the butterflies came, and story after story unfolded that my dear mother-in-law casually said one day, "You should write a book." I smiled, and said, "Yeah, maybe," thinking okay, I'll think about it. "Yeah," she said, "You could call it, Find Your Butterfly."

"Find Your Butterfly," I thought. We had just spent the afternoon discussing all the butterfly stories, and I had mentioned that it was the butterflies that got me through. It was *knowing* that Ty was still here, still by my side, loving me and guiding me that got me through my dark hours. "If only everyone had butterflies," I had said. "If every angel's parent had their own sign from their children, it would be so much easier." Indeed, it would be. I truly, honestly, genuinely believe that everyone gets signs from their loved ones that they are alright. Every child in heaven sends their parents a little something to hold on to when the nights get cold. It is up to those parents to believe it, open their eyes and see it . . . . feel it . . . . know it . . .

I also believe that children can see Jesus and His angels. I believe that their honest hearts allow them to see the things that we are too jaded to experience. We are all so logical, so scientific. It is not logical, nor is it possible to scientifically explain, how a child can **be** a butterfly. On the same side, however, it is not possible that so many "coincidences" be explained. What it all comes down to is faith. I have faith that God is here, that He hears every prayer, feels every pain and wipes away every tear I have. I have faith that Ty is happy and healthy now, and that he sends me these butterflies. I have faith that Ty lives on through Mady, and that she was sent here to me, just as Ty was, to open my eyes. I have faith . . . and without it, what would I be? What would any of us be?

Need more proof? Need more convincing stories of unbelievable "coincidences". Okay.

## Chapter 38

# EVEN MORE BUTTERFLIES!

TRAVIS'S PARENTS HAD BEEN WATCHING a beautiful piece of land that overlooked the entire town and the Mississippi River for years. They had always waited to see a "For Sale" sign, hoping that someday it would be theirs. You can imagine their excitement when, since Ty's death, that day came. As they had always planned, their first project was to erect a giant cross on the property. This 40-foot stainless steel giant can be seen from several towns, major highways and local landmarks. Its beauty is obvious as it shines in the sunlight and reflects its beautiful surroundings. Beneath it lays a roaring waterfall, and it is a truly breathtaking sight.

Since its construction in 2003, hundreds, maybe even thousands of people have visited it, many telling their own stories of faith and hope.

While constructing the cross, Travis's parents became aware of an unusual amount of winged visitors. Butterflies would swarm them as they worked, and some would take it upon themselves to stop and stay a while . . . . resting on them as they tried to work. Helen had joked that Ty was keeping her from getting anything done, and on at least one occasion she had to shoo him off and tell him he would have to go play with someone else for a while if she were to get anything accomplished.

While visiting the site one day, I myself was visited by one of these pesky little critters. The beautiful butterfly began by buzzing around me, just to make sure I saw it, I guess. It didn't take long for my heart to start pounding, and I held my shaky hand out and began to talk to it. When it landed in my hand, I think my heart stopped as the tears began to fall. I had never had a butterfly land in my hand before, much less stay there as I walked.

Travis was in a hurry to leave, and I was pleading with him for just a few more minutes. As he walked away, heading for the car, the butterfly flew out of my hand, up the hill and landed on his back pocket. It was as though the butterfly was listening to my pleas, and went to get Travis's attention and make him stay. "See," I said. "It's not time to leave yet."

I have many more butterfly stories, such as the one I experienced in summer 2003. Mady napped inside as I went outside to talk to our real estate agent. As we talked in the driveway, the sun was bright and the day was beautiful. From the corner of my eye, I saw a strange shadow on the ground and turned to look. Flying above my head, unbeknownst to me, was a butterfly. I could see its shadow swarming mine, and it began to buzz around me with great speed. I tried to stay calm so as not to make the agent think I had lost my mind.

Eventually, the butterfly flew away, and the agent left. I continued down the driveway, got the mail and headed back to the house. It was then that the same butterfly returned from the garden, and flew straight up to me. I greeted him with a "Hello," and stopped. He flew around me, and as I reached out my hand, he landed safely inside it. My heart raced, and I didn't know what to do first. Of course, the mother in me wanted to hug it, squeeze it, kiss it and rejoice. The logical adult in me said that if I were to do that, I would smash the butterfly, draw the attention of passing cars and probably be committed to a psychiatric ward somewhere.

I held the beautiful creature in my hand, and began to walk. I feared that my movement would scare it away, but it calmly stayed with me and even allowed me to sit on the porch swing.

We spent several minutes together; I talked to it as I swung, there on that same swing that had seen me through some of my best days. I had swung there with Travis just days before Ty's arrival, when my life spiraled out of control. I was there in that swing with my dear, sweet boy, on many a sunny afternoon. We would swing until we both fell asleep.

I watched it investigate my palm as it just seemed to listen to my teary conversation. It would fly away for a few seconds, buzz around me on the swing, then come back. It was a flashback to my first butterfly encounter, and it was so beautiful that I did not ever want it to end.

It was that same summer that we took Mady to the Butterfly House in St. Louis. The Butterfly house is a wonderful place. An enormous butterfly habitat is open to the public, and you can enjoy thousands of butterflies in their own environment.

While there, I wondered if Ty would give us a little "Hello." I hoped and prayed that something would happen, and it did. Travis had Mady in a backpack, and I was armed with my camera. We hadn't been inside for more than a few minutes when a couple of butterflies came by. They were chasing each other, playing, and seemed so carefree as they flew. They flew right to Travis and Mady, and began to chase each other right around their heads. It was then that one of the pair decided to take a rest on Mady's ear. I captured the humor of the event on film as Mady wiggled and cringed to the sound of fluttering in her ear. The butterfly then left her ear, and began buzzing around her head.

It was amazing, and once again I was crying. Now, do I know for sure that this was Ty? No, I don't. But, I have faith that it was. I have faith that Ty sent that butterfly to say "Hello." My faith in God, and my faith that Ty is with me is what gets me through my darkest days. The joy that Mady brings me when she stops to take a bow for a job well done fills my heart with laughter, and I know that somewhere her brother is laughing, too. I believe that when I speak to him, he listens. When I need him, he is there.

*Chapter 39*

# TY, IS THAT YOU?

WHEN MADY WAS AN INFANT, she was a terrible sleeper. She did not sleep through the night until she was 9 months old, and even that was not consistent. There was one night in particular that I found myself once again in her room to comfort her. I was rocking her to sleep, and began to recall my last time rocking Ty. The rocking motion of the glider-rocker took me straight back to the rocking of the chair in the PICU the night I rocked Ty to sleep for his final slumber. My heart began to race and I once again felt my body get hot as the tears began to fall.

As I wept and thought of all the things I would've done had I known that I was rocking him for the last time, I began to talk to him. I rocked Mady, just as I had rocked Ty, and held her close to my body as I talked to Ty. I told him the story of our last moments together as tears streamed down my face. As I spoke, I asked him if he was here and if he was listening. Just then, the nightlight went out, and the room was covered in a blanket of darkness. I must admit, I was a little spooked at first.

"Is that you?" I asked. I continued to rock, and just as suddenly as it had gone off, the light came back on. I finished my story, put a sleeping Mady back to bed, and began to leave the room. As I passed the nightlight, which now was shining brightly, I stopped to give it a good shake. I expected to find it loose in its outlet, offering an explanation to what had happened. What I found, however, was that it was not loose at all. That nightlight never flickered again.

## Chapter 40

# A PLACE WHERE I WAS 'NORMAL'

I BELIEVE WITH ALL OF my heart that every human deserves a place that makes them feel like they belong. For some, it is going to work every day at a job that they love. For those with special needs, perhaps it is going to a workshop that focuses on the things they CAN do, rather than those that they cannot. For parents of a sick child, that place is CaringBridge.

I had been following several sick children through CaringBridge for some time, which was therapeutic for me. CaringBridge.org offers free websites to the families of sick children (and adults) in order to keep family and friends updated on their progress. Some of the children I kept up with are technically strangers to me. I have never met them, and probably never will. They are all over the United States, and some are visitors from other countries, seeking healing here in the US. I would frequent these children's sites, leaving encouraging messages, never expecting to do any more than perhaps let them know that someone cares. I knew all too well the feelings of loneliness that accompany having a sick child. I felt compelled to take just a few minutes and let the parents of these children know that someone understood, and more importantly, cared.

Caringbridge allowed me to think out loud. It afforded me an outlet for the words that God would sometimes overwhelm me with. They would flood into my mind, and I could think of nothing else. Those around me had moved on with their lives. It wasn't that they didn't care, but they could not fully grasp the feelings I was experiencing. They could not wrap their minds around the life that I now called mine, but I knew that these things were happening to me so that I could share them with *someone*. CaringBridge, and the families I met there, gave me an opportunity to get those words out.

I had been on a train for 24 years. I found comfort in my seat on the train, and knew my place there. Suddenly, I had been thrust off of the train and felt a tornadic wind on my face as I plummeted to the ground with painful speed. When I came to, I found myself in an alternate universe. I existed there, in that world, along side my beautiful boy. I became accustomed to my new surroundings and began to feel at home there. Then, one day, as suddenly as I had been thrust into this world, it was taken away from me. I found myself there, bruised and battered, watching as that train whisked past me again. I could see the passengers, their faces pressed against the glass like kids at the hippo display at the zoo. They were all looking at me intently, waiting for me. They watched me, wondering why I wasn't jumping back on. They had known I had gotten off the train. They had heard the stories of the world I had uncovered, but could not fully understand it. Here I was, the train whizzing by, and suddenly I wasn't sure where I belonged. My beautiful boy was gone, and I no longer had a home in my new 'normal' world. But, equally as concerning, I no longer felt as though I belonged on the train. Its passengers were self-absorbed and worried about things like pedicures and pizza parties. They had not seen what I had seen. They had not felt what I had felt. Where did I belong? They all watched me as they zoomed by, expecting me to run and reach my desperate hand out for the handle and pull myself up. I found myself unsure of whether I could ever relate to the other passengers again. The train had kept going while I had been in my alternate universe. The passengers had gone on without me, and life went on. They could not speak my new language, and I wasn't sure I could ever go back to speaking theirs. CaringBridge helped me see that I *could* get back on the train. I *should* get back on the train. I didn't have to go back to my old seat. I didn't even have to go back to the same car. I simply had to find the courage to make the jump, and God would help me find a car full of passengers who spoke my language.

Eventually, I started my own CaringBridge page in Ty's memory, and it served as a huge part of my healing process. It was there, in the land of CaringBridge, that I learned that people could care about the things I had to say, even if they didn't know me. They understood the dialect I spoke that most others found foreign. I could go there any time I wanted, and let out all of the words and thoughts, fears and concerns that would flood my mind. Though I now had Mady, and she was a wonderful light in the dark for me; I still had power outages from time to time. Times when my memories of Ty would overwhelm me, and I just needed to 'belong.' Travis just couldn't talk about his grief, so I felt all alone inside my cocoon of sadness sometimes. CaringBridge solved that for me. In fact, it was there that I received some of my first encouragements to write this book.

Now, years later, I have gone back to re-read some of the journal entries I made there, in my safe-place; the place where I could speak freely, and know that I would be understood. In reading them, I have decided to include some of them here, in the hopes that maybe they would serve as a helping hand for you, too.

The following is a message I had left for a couple who had recently lost their 1-year-old son to a terrible disease. I hope that in reading it, even if you have never lost a child, you will somehow find something to hold on to when the lights go out, and you, too, feel alone.

My message read:

***When the lights finally go down for the night, the television is off and all is quiet . . . we think of our children who have gone before us.***

*We wonder why they have gone, and when we will see them, hold them, smell them and kiss them once more.*

*When the sun comes up, and the day is new . . . we think of our children who have gone before us. We wonder if it is them that makes the day so sweet, the sun so bright and the butterflies fly. We talk to them, remind them of our eternal love, and send them kisses, wishes and dreams up to their high home.*

*When the day gets long, and traffic is thick, that song comes on and we think of our children who have gone before us. Those memories come flooding back, of pumps that beep, monitors that alarm and big doors that close behind us. It is painful to remember, but more painful to forget.*

*What is most important through these days is NEVER to forget the love we felt when all those things happened. God handed us something more precious than those noises, pains and fears . . . he handed us life. He did not send a warranty package, a return policy or an owner's manual. They did not come with an expiration date . . . .*

*If they would have, would we have taken them?*

*I know I would have. Reluctantly at first I am sure, but my son was worth one minute with him on earth. I know Noah was, too.*

*Just remember when the days get long, and the nights longer . . . and you feel as though God has left you there to die . . . He is there, and so is Noah--They will both hold you, love you, and lead you where you need to go.*

*I am praying daily for God to send you a little one . . . one with Noah's eyes, his spirit and his love. That child will come, but we must all be patient.*

*Know that you are not forgotten, and neither is Noah.*

Allowing these words to flow through me started a wildfire of inspiration for this book. Unknowingly, I was allowing God to speak *to* me, and speak *through* me.

I had left these parents messages before, and have been praying for God to answer their wish to have another child, a healthy child. This message was no different. I simply wished for them to know that I had been in their shoes, and give them hope that they would survive it just as I had.

The day following my message, I received an email from another parent who had visited the site and read my message. "It was as though you had looked right into my heart," she said, as she spoke of her beloved son. Shawn lost her beloved son, Reese, in March of 2003, and found her own feelings in my message. She asked if she could post my message onto Reese's site, so that Reese's visitors could read it and understand how she had been feeling.

I was flattered. I was flabbergasted. I was in utter shock that someone had read my message and found some kind of comfort in it. I immediately wrote Shawn back, and told her I would be honored if she would post my message on Reese's site. I explained briefly my experiences with Ty, and that I had begun writing a book but never finished.

Little did I know that I was about to find myself overwhelmed with a drive I had not felt in a while. Within a day, Shawn had posted my message on Reese's site. Below it she explained how she had come across the message, and gave the readers what information she had on Ty. She ended by saying:

*Ok - Reesie Cup fans and for the beautiful poem. Who is this Jennifer? Well, she's a lady I just met online thru Noah's website. She left this message in his guestbook. I contacted her to see if she would allow me to post these beautiful words on Reese's site. She wrote me back and said she would be honored. She also shared with me a little about herself - how she lost a son at 3 1/2 months, and how she began writing a book. Don't you agree with me that she should definitely continue? You think this is good? Read the poem she wrote to her son on his 2nd birthday in the guestbook.*

*Thank you, Jennifer, for allowing me to share your words.*

That sparked something within me that I found overwhelming. I couldn't believe that she had taken my message so to heart. More unbelievable was that she took the time to write me about it, and then actually posted my message for others to read.

Shawn wrote me again with more personal information on her life in the past year, and I found myself feeling as though I had known her forever. I felt a connection to her, to Reese, to her life.

Within another 24 hours, I received several more emails from other parents, encouraging me to finish my book, explaining how my words had captured their thoughts. How was this possible? Why was this happening? I knew that God had gotten impatient with me and decided to take matters into his own hands to get me kicked into gear.

I received a beautiful message from another mother named Kim, whose son Kody has a very rare brain tumor. She asked me to drop a few lines to a dear friend of hers who had just lost her daughter. "Me?" She wanted ME to say something to help this mother? I cannot explain the honor that I felt. I was being invited into the most personal, painful moments of these mothers' lives. Me.

Explain that with logic. There is no explanation. What God has given me in those five short days had driven me to write this book. What Shawn, Kim and the other mothers that wrote me did for me is beyond measure.

They reminded me that Ty has a story. He has a story that deserves to be told. By telling that story, I am not only honoring him, but embodying the lives of other parents as well. God puts these words into my head. These words come from my heart, and I cannot explain the overwhelming nature by which they come. When these thoughts, these memories come into my mind, they take over my head. I find myself unable to sleep, unable to concentrate on other things until I write them. I know that God and Ty are pushing me, and that they are the source of these words.

For that I am truly thankful, for in five short days, I had not only worked on this book, but had made friends with whom I share a personal bond.

We are all mothers . . . mothers who love our children unconditionally, and long to hold them once more. That bond's strength is beyond measure. We may never meet face to face, but we don't need to, for we have met heart to heart, and that is much stronger.

Thank you, Shawn and Kim, Reese and Kody.

**The following is an excerpt from Ty's CaringBridge site, that beautiful place where I could be myself. A place where death of a child did not make you stand out; rather, it allowed you to be part of the family.**

**Tuesday, August 10, 2004 9:42 AM CDT**

*Last night, as I lay in bed alone, thinking of today, and what it may hold . . .*

*I couldn't help but think about the ways my life has changed since August 10, 2001.*

*I thought of the blessings that have come my way, the sorrow, the heart-ache, and the hardships. I thought of how my life could've been, how it would've been had Ty not died, or had he never been born, and the person I could've been.*

*These thoughts are not ones that I encounter daily, or even weekly or monthly. No longer do I dwell upon the could've beens and should've beens on a regular basis--No, it takes a special day to conjure up such thoughts. Of course, last night I had much on my mind. Between anticipating the third anniversary of Ty's death, and pondering some news my mom gave me yesterday, my imagination bounced around from thing to thing, topic to topic like a bouncing ball. As some of you may know, my mom has been fighting breast cancer. This week actually marks the 1st anniversary of when she was diagnosed, and about 4 months ago she completed her chemotherapy. Bald, puffy and filled with chemicals, she was then informed that she would need radiation and a mastectomy--something she was not really told in the beginning. She has fought with her conscience for these past few months, trying to decide whether or not to undergo more brutal abuse. She did not embrace the idea of scarring her already beaten body with a mastectomy, much less filling herself with radiation--so she's sought several second opinions, all leading her down the same road. With a mastectomy scheduled for next Monday, the 16th, she found a new lump in her breast on Sunday. A blow to her esteem that she tried to blow off, I know her mind must be racing. Wondering if she's waited too long to undergo the last leg of her treatment, wondering if this lump will be the end . . . wondering.*

*These developments left me wondering last night, too. Lying there alone, the tears began to fall as I thought of what the real world has brought to me in the past few years. It seems as though God has thrown many hurdles before me, waiting to see if I can jump them consecutively without falling flat on my face and skidding for yards and yards before I admit defeat. However, these hurdles placed before me have forced me to become a stronger, more faithful person. I would like to think that I am a more upbeat, positive person as well. I do not dwell on these obstacles, I simply grin and try to cross them the best I can. Please do not misconstrue this journal as negative, for it is not meant in that way. I'm simply venting on this crappy anniversary that has been given to me, that of my sweet baby boy's death. It's one of those days where it seems appropriate to complain and whine a little . . . and then move on.*

*The real world hit me for the first time in about November of 2000 when Ty was diagnosed in utero with all of the heart problems that would eventually take him from me on the day before my own 25th birthday, August 10th, 2001. The following year, on my wedding anniversary, September 16th, my sister-in-law lost her precious son, Devin . . . who was still born at full term. The next year, the week of my birthday, my mom was diagnosed with cancer . . . the news of which I received by telephone either on the anniversary of Ty's death, or on my birthday--I can't exactly remember which. So, this year, for my birthday, I receive the news that the cancer which could not be detected in her body just*

*4 months ago is back, rearing its ugly head in the form of a lump . . . just a week before the dreaded mastectomy is to be performed.*

*It's funny, somehow, how so many things can happen during the times in your life that are supposed to render elation and celebration--isn't it? Birthdays and anniversaries become of little importance when surrounded, or rather drowned, by death and cancer. It's one of those realizations that come about when you officially become an adult. As children, there is nothing more sacred than birthdays . . . anticipation of parties filled with piñatas, pin the tail on the donkey and mountainous cakes covered with candles that re-light themselves. Kids cheering, wrapping paper flying, just thinking of it makes you smell the extinguished candles and get those butterflies in your stomach that always appeared the night before the party.*

*Then 'life' gets in the way, adult decisions, eternal consequences and real world issues . . . and before you know it, childhood is gone, taking with it all the wonder and mystery that used to accompany such coveted occasions.*

*My only sibling, my brother Marty, is going to be a senior in high school this year. I was just preaching at him (uninvited preaching, I may add) at how he needs to cherish these times, enjoy them, get in a little trouble for once, and just LIVE . . . before the real world comes and swallows him up. I know he worries too much about our mom, her outcome, and life in general already for his young age of 17. I told him of how quickly the world snuck up on me, raining on my youthful parade. It seems like yesterday I was graduating from high school. I moved out by age 19 to escape our controlling dad, and was suddenly running a household, going to college and working. Life was wonderful. I was an adult. Then, bam, somehow by 24 my Cheerios had been peed in, I was having a baby that was very sick, and from there, you know the scenario. It's funny how quickly things happen, isn't it?*

*So, last night, the tears saturated my pillow as I thought of all these things. They swirled in my mind, as did others, and I came to a sudden realization.* **As I asked God for strength today, I asked Him to let Ty visit me, if only for a moment, just to let me know he was okay, and I found myself** *talking to God as though he sat on the bed with me. Telling him things he already knew, I made myself feel better, somehow, and thought of something I wanted to share with all of you today.*

I didn't intend to cry on your shoulder for so long today, actually, but it just came out. So, let me get to the point that I was trying to make 5 paragraphs ago . . .

Last night, it occurred to me that all of us get dealt crappy hands occasionally. The true test, it seems, is not actually the hurdle, but how you choose to cross it. God creates the hurdle, designed especially for you, but He gives you Free Will when it comes to your way of handling it. You can back up, get a run at it, and leap across with strength and endurance you hadn't known before. You can cross it slowly, one leg at a time, weak and frail. You can cower, crawling underneath the hurdle, refusing to try your hand at jumping. Or, you can completely refuse to try; surrendering to the challenge and falling to your knees at the base of such an obstacle . . . never even attempting to overcome it.

It is this truth that mystifies me. The different ways that such similarly made humans can opt to deal with life's obstacles. Free Will is so mysterious. As I explore the CaringBridge world, meeting so many different families, with different obstacles, different worlds, different challenges . . . . I see the similarities that bind us, yet the differences that separate us. Families lose children here daily, as though it is 'normal', and here there is a sense of protection and community provided to families that just don't jive in the 'normal' world anymore. And though we all have so much in common, we are handling things so differently.

God deals everyone challenges, opportunities to strengthen ourselves. Sometimes it is the loss of a job, sometimes it is a business opportunity--and sometimes it is the illness or death of a child. It is not pleasant, but it is fact. Some people do not share my view, feeling as though God is out to get them or punish them in some way, and cannot find anything positive in the illness of a child. I am not saying that it is easy, or pleasant to have a sick kid . . . don't get me wrong. But I'm saying you have to FIND the positive inside of *the negative, find the piece God places inside you that allows you to grow and become stronger. So many people don't do that. They cower at the foot of the mountain, refusing to even try to climb it . . . forgetting that if they would just stand and rise to the challenge, God would lift them to the top, allowing them to stand in glory at what they had achieved for themselves. I really believe that if you stand and tell Him that you will try your best, you will be open to challenge, open to learning, open to his lesson-He will not allow you to fail. Sure, it seems like failure when you must bury your beloved child, unable to have healed them within the conventional sense of the word, unable to keep them on earth with you. Sure, that seems like defeat.*

*But, somehow, it is not. God doesn't give us the entire plan, we don't get a copy of that book. But, I know in my heart that it exists, and our children are a huge part of it, and for that, we should be thankful. Thankful to have known them, if only for a day. Thankful to have felt them within our souls, thankful to have been allowed to call them ours. It doesn't matter how long they were 'ours', it matters that they WERE ours at all . . . for now they are HIS, and that is truly an honor.*

*So, today, as I think of my little monkey, and the brief time I had with him on Earth--I also think of all the time I'll have with him someday, the stories we will share, and the blessings he has brought me. He has taught me so many things, though he was only here 3 ½ months, and I continue to learn from him. In fact, I did last night.*

**I learned that God's plan is final, regardless of what I want. I learned that God's love is eternal, regardless of how I screw up. Most of all, I learned that I am Ty's mom, and always will be . . . regardless of his current address.**

*May you also be blessed with such lessons from your children, lessons from God . . . . lessons of love, loss and challenge. For they are what make us grow, make us real, make us human.*

## Chapter 41

# AFTER THE HURRICANE, COMES A RAINBOW

FOR YEARS, AUGUST 10 REPRESENTED darkness for me. The day before my birthday; and birthdays becoming less and less exciting as years passed, Ty's death and my mom's cancer had pretty well made the entire month of August suck! Our nephew, Devin's death created pain on my wedding anniversary, September 16, and I began to feel like never trying to celebrate again!

That is, until 2006. Pregnant with baby # 3, I was due the first week of August. Having had Ty one week early, and Mady two weeks early, I assumed this baby would come in late July. I can remember going to the doctor, and having him tell me that perhaps we should explore the option of inducing. 'Yeah, whatever', I thought. 'My babies come early, no need for that.' I remember vaguely him mentioning something about reserving a room for me at the hospital, just in case. Honestly, I sort of tuned him out, knowing full well that he was being paranoid.

Well, I spent my due date eating pizza at the jobsite with Travis . . .

Hmmmmm . . . . that's weird. No baby. Maybe I should have paid more attention when Dr. Lange was talking about inducing me. I went back for my last visit, and this time, I actually listened to what he said. He had already booked that room . . . on August 10. I thought surely I would go into labor on my own, just as I had each time before, and I wouldn't need that silly room.

But I didn't. So, on August 10, 2006, Travis and I headed to the hospital. I couldn't help but laugh, really, because as soon as they started the process of induction, labor came easily. This baby seemed to be playing with me, messing with me! It went so fast, in fact, that just about the time I started to consider needing an epidural, I suddenly needed to push! Holy cow! The poor Anesthesiologist was rushing to get me some pain relief so that I could deliver! In fact, Dr. Lange barely made it in the door. He rushed to my bed, started to dress for delivery, and said something that made me laugh . . . .

And that was it! I laughed out a healthy baby boy. The poor doc didn't even have time to finish dressing. Whoops!

Jacob Cole Naeger entered the world surrounded by laughter. Healthy, beautiful, and screaming. Just the way I had hoped. And from that day on, August 10 became a little happier. Again, some pessimists could call this coincidence. But, really? 365 days in a year to deliver, and this kid refuses to come out until August 10? A whole week past the due date? Yeah. I'm not buying it!

## Chapter 42

# PRICE CHECK ON AISLE 4

So, I OFTEN WONDER HOW other people get through life. Muddling through, unhappy, stressed and out of touch with the TRUE meaning of life. Consumed by wants and 'needs', overwhelmed with desires, unreachable goals and the pursuit of all things material. Yet, sometimes, I find myself doing the same.

What grounds me, though, is the tie that binds me to the true meaning of life. Like those little coily rubber ties that people put their key rings on, and then hook them to their beltloop or around their wrist; I have a similar, though invisible, tie. It connects me to my truth, much like an umbilical cord attaches a child to its mother. Though I can't see it, I can feel it. It is attached to my soul, and occasionally, I become too 'human' for my own good, and stretch it beyond its capacity. It is then that it fully extends, and snaps me like a slingshot back to center. Like the sound of a whip cracking in the wind, sometimes it surprises me.

We all recall the first time we got separated from our parents at the store. One minute, you felt safe and carefree. In an instant, you turn to find that everyone familiar is gone. The panic sets in so quickly, and immediately your mind begins to wander to the what- ifs. What if they have forgotten me and left? What if I never find my way back to them, and I am alone forever? What if? What if?

Much like that child, we all wander too far away sometimes. We allow the worries of the world to carry us far, far away. Before we know it, we turn around and can find nothing that gives us comfort and security; everything looks different and we worry that we will never find our way back.

That child inside of us could not rationalize that our parents would not leave us. It always turned out that they were one aisle over, testing us to teach us a lesson about staying close and being observant and careful. In the same way, God stands and waits for us now, as adults. He gives us Free Will to wander away, to stray from His side. But He never goes more than one aisle over. He continues to peek through the stacks of canned peas and toilet paper, watching us as we turn to discover that we have wandered too far. He watches, and He waits. He, just like our parents, hopes that we will feel that panic, and learn a life-lesson from it. That we will never forget the way the lump feels in our throat as we realize that we are seemingly all alone and frightened. As the sounds of the price check on aisle 4 on the overhead speaker begin to muffle, our hearts beat fast and our vision becomes blurred through tears and we become desperate to find our safe place again . . . He is there . . .

*Chapter 43*

# GETTING IN THE CAB, AND LETTING THAT CRAZY GUY DRIVE!

N OW, LOOK. I REALIZE THAT from the time you were 3 years old, your mother has warned you to NEVER get in the car with a stranger!! But work with me here!

I have a simple philosophy to the way I handle my life now.

Let's imagine you were alone for a business meeting in a large city. Left without a vehicle, and needing to make it to your meeting, you would have two choices.

A. You could walk to the meeting alone, guessing at the correct path. It would be dangerous, and would take quite some time to get there. Unfamiliar with the area, you could easily take a wrong turn and get off track. Every city has streets that are on 'the wrong side of the tracks', places where even a good person can get in trouble. Without knowing *where* they are, how on earth will you know how to avoid them?

There would be intersections to cross, seemingly helpless against all of the large cars that zoom past. There would be puddles to leap over, hills to climb . . . . and here you are: ALONE.

Or . . . . There's plan B.

You could choose to take a cab. This would be a much quicker trip, and would allow the opportunity of traveling with someone familiar with the area. Sure, some cab drivers can be scary. Heck, I've been in a cab before where the guy driving wasn't even the same guy whose photo was taped to the dash! You just might find yourself at the mercy of some crazy guy, putting your trust in someone you have never met before. But I have learned that letting the crazy guy drive is always a better approach than going out into the world alone, and hoping for the best! He knows which roads are closed for construction, which detours should be taken, and the fastest route to your destination. It's his job!

**This is my approach to letting go; which in essence, allows me to gain MORE control!** I have learned that I *can* do things my way (damned Free Will!)

I can fight over that steering wheel, and take the path I want to take. I picture a scene in a movie: Riding in a car, tires squalling, passing cars honking. Weaving all over the road in and out of traffic as I reach over, yanking the wheel with passion. Determined to gain control because I think I can do it better; I put myself in great danger.

Or, I can allow God (the crazy guy) to drive, and shut up and put on my seatbelt. He doesn't usually take the same route I would've, and sometimes that annoys the heck out of me. Most of the time He refuses to hit the Starbucks drive-thru on the way, and that REALLY bugs me. Sometimes He wants to take the scenic route and show me the sites, really hoping it will help me grow along the way. Other times He drives so fast, and takes such a direct route that I am really not ready to get out of the car when we get there . . . because I'm scared.

Regardless of which route He takes, one thing is always the same. When He gets me there, He always rushes to my side of the car. He kindly opens my door, and lovingly extends His hand. And as soon as I get the courage to put my hand into His, I know that I can do it. Whatever it is, no matter how insurmountable it seems, I know that it can be done. It doesn't mean I'm not scared of the journey, it simply means that I am as ready as I will ever be because He is the one in control . . . and I'm just along for the ride.

My wish for you, my intention with writing this book, is that you too will be able to find YOUR savior. I cannot predict what form He will take when He nudges you because God likes to spice things up! I don't know how long your journey to our common destination will be. If I find out He took you through the Starbucks drive-thru, I admit, I will be mad! But what I do know is that He will, undoubtedly, when you have reached your destination, open your door and extend His hand for yours. I hope that after traveling this road with me you can open your eyes to His gentle nudges, and place your hand in His so that He can help you. Open your heart, your ears, and your mind as you read and try to find YOUR savior as you read about mine. If for no other reason, do it so that he doesn't have to resort to whacking you in the back of the skull with a shovel to get your attention!

# Chapter 44

# HELLO . . . . IS THIS THING ON??

S O, DID YOU EVER HEAR that joke about the lady who gets stuck in a flood? The water rises until she finds herself on the roof of her home, water racing by her, carrying all of her belongings off into the distance. A man in a rowboat came by and offered to take her to shore, but she refused, claiming that she was sure God would save her.

Waters continued to rise, and another boat passed, again offering her a ride. Once again, she refused, still holding out for God's miracle.

Finally, a helicopter hovered over her, offering to throw down a ladder to save her life, but a third time she refused the help. Shortly after, the water swept her away and she met her demise. Reaching Heaven, and feeling pretty disgusted, she asked God why He had forsaken her, as she held on to her faith until the bitter end? He looked puzzled at her, and replied, "Well, I sent you two boats and a helicopter, what more do you want from me?"

Yeah, so, I am pretty sure I have reached helicopter status with God at this point.

For what seems like an eternity now, I have been praying for God to touch my heart. I've begged, I've pleaded, I've bugged Him to death.

"Please, touch my heart and tell me what I am supposed to be doing. Tell me what I can do. What I was put here to do. What your intended purpose is for me. If you tell me, I will do it. I promise. Just tell me. Talk loud. Scream it. Jump up and down in the middle of the road. But . . . . TELL ME! PLEASE!

I can just envision Him up there shaking His head at me. The only thing I can say is that He is the one that made me this way . . . so in a way He should share some of the blame for my inability to listen properly!!

If there is one thing I have learned through the experiences of the past ten years, it is that God has created me with a purpose. With each challenge I undergo, with each hurdle I climb, no matter how poorly I may do so, and despite my lack of athletic ability-there is something to be learned. I have a choice, and must make a conscious effort to make the correct choice; to see that God does not do things TO me, He does things FOR me. I have learned, throughout this awakening process that the more in tune I am with Him, the smoother things go.

Yet, despite this knowledge, I am here to tell you that I, of all people, have been dragging my feet unknowingly. Ten years ago, He sent me a wake up call. I acknowledged it, learned from it, grew from it, and embraced it for all that it was. Then, He sent me messengers. Multiple people supplying me with encouragement to use a gift that He had sent me. Did I do it? Well, I started to. I did it for a while, then I stopped. I listened, then I tuned it out. I turned on the gift, then I let the light go out. The whole time, I thought I was still listening. It was like leaving the radio on, but turning the volume off, and thinking you were still technically listening! Come on! I know better than this . . . *right?*

Yeah, apparently not! For several years now, I have been *hearing* without listening! So, here I am praying every day, several times a day, for Him to speak to me. I have felt like a slacker, because 10 years have passed since that wake up call. He reached in and pulled the string that turned the light bulb on, and I have known that there was some divine purpose He sent it to me . . . but I haven't delivered. I've racked my brain, I've gone round and round . . . NOTHING!

'Just give it more time' I thought. 'Maybe it's not the right time yet . . . ' That was my excuse. I see that now. Here I was praying for Him to beat me over the head with the answer, and the whole time He is doing just that and I keep blaming it on the wind!

It started with encouragement to write a book. I started, and it was such a healing process for me. But, as I felt more and more adjusted, I let it go. I stopped working on the book, and writing on Ty's CaringBridge page. Somehow, I got consumed in daily life, and here I am, ten years later with nothing but some words on some pages that were never completed. Those initial words flowed out of me like water from a faucet, and I knew then that it was exactly what I was supposed to be doing. Much like a songwriter says that a song just comes to them, those words came into my heart, and out through my fingers, and I knew I was in 'the zone.' But when the zone left me, I let the words stop. And I waited . . . and waited . . . . and waited.

As time has gone on, there have been gentle nudges from God. Small reminders that I had started something and not finished it. Kind of like how a parent gently asks a child, "Isn't it your turn to do the dishes???" and then waits for them to step up to the plate and do the chore. Yeah, God has been sitting around waiting for me to do the dishes for so long, those suckers stink and are now piled across the counter! And still, He was patient.

The big nudge came in the last couple of months, via two different 'nudgers'. The first happened at church (shocking, right?). Part of the Catholic mass is for the priest to offer us the peace of our Lord, to which we reply, 'And also, with you.' At this time, we then turn to others around us and offer them peace, by shaking hands.

It was an unassuming Sunday, nothing particularly special. As is tradition, during the sign of peace, we all turned to one another and shook hands. Normally, the saying is simply, "Peace be with you", or even simpler yet, "Peace". This day, though, something strange happened. It was an innocent enough situation, simply shaking hand with another parishioner. A woman in front of me, someone I do not know, turned to me and smiled, and extended her hand. I smiled back, and whispered, "Peace", as I kindly placed my right hand into hers, then laying my left hand on top. I do this as my way of showing I mean my granting of the Lord's peace upon them sincerely, rather than just flopping my hand carelessly into theirs and throwing out the word "Peace" like I was saying 'Pass the ketchup.' So, here we were, hands intertwined, when she threw the curveball. What she said to me caught me so off-guard, I spent the rest of the mass inside of my own head, rather than paying attention, replaying her words. She looked me straight in the eye, her face illuminated and her eyes smiling brightly, and said "Peace be with *all* of you, because YOU'RE the one that wrote the book."

Whoa! This is not what we are supposed to say! 'What the heck does that mean?', I thought. To this day, if I allow myself to stew on it long enough, I can convince myself that I must have misunderstood. Surely that isn't what she said. I must be going crazy. I replayed the words in my head throughout church, trying to break it down and come up with an alternate phrase. She must have said something else, like . . . . ummmmm . . . . "Peace be with all of you, because you're the one who threw the rock???" ". . . because you're the one whose road it took?" Crap! No matter how I change it, it doesn't make sense! I told Travis about it once we got to the car, my mind still reeling. He, of course, told me it was because I WAS supposed to be writing a book, and followed it with that know-it-all thing kids usually do: "*Seeeeeeeeeeeee???????????*" Geez, thanks, Pal! That really helped!

It was within a couple of months that I got my bigger nudge. It was one that I really wanted to blow off as coincidence, if it weren't for the fact that I don't actually *believe* in coincidence; something that sometimes ticks me off about myself! I had the extreme blessing of finding someone very dear to me through my newest favorite form of news and information: Facebook. I had located my beloved friend, the Pediatric Nurse, Amy, whom had been with us the night he died. She loved him as if he were her own child, and she will forever be the owner of a large piece of my heart.

She and I had learned shortly after his death that we were both pregnant that final day, there inside that Pediatric ICU, though neither of us was the wiser. With myself having a critically ill newborn and herself actually having an infant she was nursing, neither of us *should* have been pregnant. Yet, somehow, we both had little girls within 5 days of one another. And that was just the beginning of our similarities!

Amy and I arranged to meet for lunch one Sunday afternoon to catch up. We had not done this for about 8 years, so it was far overdue. As we sat down together over a margarita, it didn't take long for the question to pop out of her mouth. "Did you ever publish that book?" Oy! Seriously? "No," I said. "I worked on it for a while, and it just sort of stopped." She and I had talked about this when our girls were just one year old, and she had even offered to write down her part of Ty's story, and what it meant to her, as an insert to the book. *Nudge, nudge,* I thought. Ugh, why couldn't I just believe in coincidence, and ignore it?? I hear you, God. I hear you!

Well . . . NO MORE EXCUSES!! I had to make this book happen! I mean, He sent me two boats and a helicopter. What more did I want?

# Chapter 45

# I'M NOT LISTENING . . .
# I <u>DON'T WANT TO!</u>

S O, HERE I AM PRAYING for some kind of divine intervention. I know full well that I was created with a purpose in mind. God does not just willy-nilly create us, with no intention.

Even though it seems like perhaps He just got bored one day, and went on a wild rampage where he created things like mosquitoes and poison ivy with no actual plan, I know that this is not the case. Rest assured, I actual keep a perpetual list of questions I fully intend to ask when I arrive at Heaven's Gate someday, and these little nuggets are on the list! As I have been talking with Mady, now 9 years old, about God's plans, His expectations, and how to fulfill them, it occurred to me that I was being a hypocrite. I was not practicing what I preached, or at least not to my full potential.

I truly believe, with every fiber of my being, that when God created me, He had a goal for me. He molded me by hand, and had dreams and expectations for me. However, He also provided me with Free Will, something I really wonder if He sometimes kicks Himself for! (Yes . . . . this one is on my list, too!) Free Will is the thing that gets us into trouble. He did not want to create robots, doing as they were commanded and with a lack of passion. He created us with a purpose, and then provided us with Free Will . . . then sent us off into the world, filled with hope that we would *choose* to fulfill that goal. Like any parent, He loves us despite our flaws, our poor decisions and all of our fumbles along the way. But, rather than do the work *for* us, He allows us to make our own path, and sits patiently, fingers crossed that we will ASK for help, PRAY for guidance, and do our BEST to choose the path He wants us to choose.

Mady and I talked about this, too. I explained to her that God created each of us, and sent us out into the world. But, as soon as we get here, we get all arrogant and start thinking WE are in control; that it's OUR life to live, and that WE should make all of the decisions. So, as humans, that is what we do. Much like a lab rat, we wander aimlessly through that stupid maze, while someone watches on from above, and repeatedly ram our heads into the wall and wonder why it doesn't help. Really? THAT seems like a good idea? As we do this, our friends and family unknowingly encourage this behavior by telling us that it's part of being human to make mistakes. They tell us that it's part of growing up to be lost, and that we will figure it out. No one ever told me growing up that there was an easier way. So, I feel an obligation to tell my kids, and you, so that you can tell your kids, and your mailman, and the lady at church, and that weird guy that sits next to you on the bus. There is, in fact, an easier way!

Sure, it's not fool-proof. Sadly, there is no 'Easy' button, like the ones in the commercials. It does not come with a little certificate that declares that you are guaranteed not to experience hardship, pain or suffering. But what it does come with is a guarantee that when those times come, you will not be alone. To me, that's as much as I can hope for.

## Chapter 46

# THAT DAMNED FREE WILL!

IT WASN'T UNTIL I WAS an adult that I began to understand that I did not have to be obsessive compulsive with my prayers. I was not in direct control of the fate of my family and friends, and if I fell asleep while praying, or forgot someone on my 'list', God would not punish me by allowing something horrible to happen. Prayer is important. I truly believe God provides miracles in direct response to our prayers. BUT, I know now that He isn't just sitting there with his finger on the "Disaster" button, waiting to push it if I forget something in my prayers.

I truly believe now that every decision I make, whether it be in choosing what words and tone to use while disciplining my kids, or whether or not to hold the door for the grouchy man entering behind me at the grocery store, has direct consequences. It is not only the big decisions that have a ripple effect; it is also the miniscule. I do my best to show kindness even when I am tempted not to, though I know sometimes I undoubtedly could do better. I understand now, through trial and error, that if I consult with God in everything that I do, my life goes smoother.

I don't wait until I have a problem to pray, and I don't wait for life-altering decisions to consult with Him. You see, if He created me with an intention in mind, who am I to try to call all of the shots? Wouldn't it just make more sense for me to turn to Him and say, "Okay, what do you want me to do here?" I'm not saying I am perfect, or that I never do something I wish that I hadn't. But I have come to learn that He will never misguide me, so why in the world do I run around like a crazy person trying to do it all alone? That's like parking on a hill and not using your parking brake, and instead just hoping for the best. Would you do that?

It's that darn Free Will that screws us every time. You see, God didn't want to FORCE us to love Him. He didn't want to MAKE us do the right thing. So, He created us with intention, and then sent us out to see what we would do. I know people who think that if God created us with a plan in mind, then He must have an exact course for us, and that they are in no way in control. Therefore, they refuse to take responsibility for some things that most of us consider to be common sense. They don't wear a seat belt, for example, because they say, "Well, if God intends for me to die today, wearing a seat belt isn't going to change that . . ." OH MY GRAVY! Seriously? Well, if that's the case, maybe I should just walk right out into traffic and assume that if I get hit, that's because God had me marked on his calendar of people to "off" today! COME ON!!

Take some responsibility here, people! I'm telling you, it's that stinking Free Will that has made us all morons! We have Free Will to do stupid things. God doesn't *want* us to do stupid things. He doesn't set us up to fail. But He gave us Free Will, which in turn allows us to make the wrong decisions, which snow-ball into more bad decisions, which lead us, just like those lab rats, into this dead-end where we continually beat our heads against the wall until we are no longer able to think straight. THEN . . . . we blame Him for our stupidity, and assume that it was part of His plan. I can't imagine how frustrated He must get with us. Much like we can see our children making mistakes as they grow, and we allow them to do so because we know they must make their own path in life and learn from their mishaps; God must watch us and sometimes think, "OH MY, ummm, ME! WHAT are you doing it that way for?" But, if He were to reach down here and pick us up, dust us off and set us on the right track, how would we ever learn? What would make us different from a robot, programmed to perform an intended task? So, instead, He sits up there, like a cheerleader, rooting for us, knowing full well we are going to mess up more than we are going to triumph. Why? Because that's what a loving parent does.

SO, now that we know this, why would we NOT make Him silent partner in every aspect of our lives? Why would we not choose to LISTEN to Him, to FEEL His gentle nudges? I believe so very strongly, from personal experience, that He is constantly giving us a tiny tap on the shoulder to aid us in our decisions. He will not do it for us, just as our parent could not get on that bike and ride it for us once the training wheels were removed. Instead, they ran behind us, holding on to the seat to steady us, and when the time was right, they gently let go . . . and watched, peeking through their fingers, to see if we would crash.

Now that I have opened my eyes, my heart, my mind, my soul, and my body to His nudges . . . well, things seem to be a lot smoother. I look at it like this: He spends all day watching the beautiful children he molded by hand make horrible decisions. As parents, we all have times when we learn that our children have made a poor decision. But, imagine for just a moment, if you were able to WATCH it unfold. Can you imagine watching as your child commits a murder? Can you imagine seeing your child commit adultery, while watching your other child abuse an innocent baby? What would you do, if you had to see with your own eyes the things that He sees us do? If you did that on a daily basis, and were constantly having your heart broken by your children, what would it mean to you to have one, just ONE, come to you and ask, "What should I do? What is the right decision here? Can you guide me?"

You would rejoice, that's what you would do! If He put me here, and He has a plan for me, who am I to ignore that plan and go off and do my own thing? Yet, time and time again, that is what we do. And then, we wonder why it's not working! It's no different than a person who chooses an occupation based on pay scale, and then wonders why they are unfulfilled. Years go by, and their home life suffers because despite the great pay, they just aren't happy. The world around them crumbles, but the paychecks keep coming, and rather than taking a step back and thinking, "Why is this happening? What can I do to change the course?", they just keep banging their head on that wall. Seriously? This makes sense? You can blame that on God all you want, but He is just sitting there, waiting for you to ask. It's the difference between having a mother who drives you crazy trying to tell you how to live your life, and having a mother who sits by and lets you screw up, her gentle hands folded in her lap, wishing that you would ask for advice. Telling you what to do, forcing it down your throat, would do nothing but cause you to rebel. But, waiting for you to ask, and then providing you with the gentle encouragement you need to succeed? Well, that's all it takes. He is just sitting there, waiting. Cheering you on, and probably occasionally covering His eyes because He just can't look anymore.

Sure, sometimes I get caught up in the day-to-day activities, and I tune Him out. I'm not saying I'm perfect, here. I don't mean to, it just happens. It happens to everyone. It's like driving down the road with kids arguing in the backseat. You spend the first 10 minutes telling them to stop, and after a while, you just give up and tune them out! It happens to the best of us, but it's so much easier to just speak honestly to God and ask Him to speak as loudly as He needs to in order for us to hear Him.

So, shut up, stop thinking you are in control, and just surrender. I mean, seriously, is YOUR WAY really working? What do you have to lose?

*Chapter 47*

# CALL IT WHAT YOU WANT...

I KNOW PEOPLE WHO FEEL they need proof that God exists in order to fully believe. I know others who say that they are spiritual, but not religious. I look at it like this:

*Just as a mother knows a child is within her womb, I know that God is in my heart. A mother cannot see inside of herself to view that child with her eyes, but she can feel it move within her. She cannot physically touch it, yet she knows that it is there, living, breathing. I cannot see God with my eyes, but I can feel His touch. I cannot see His hand as He extends it toward me, but I can feel Him take my hand and lead me.*

I know with every fiber of myself that He is with me every second of every day. I also know that there must be a reason that He *chose* me to be Ty's mother. Of all the people in the world, He chose me. He did not do this *TO* me, He did this *FOR* me. I know that Ty was given to me for a reason. I was chosen to be his mother, and him to be my child. God has a plan for me, something I am to fulfill, and I owe it to Him to do whatever He wants me to do. Without Ty, what kind of person would I be? Would I be as close to God? Would I be here at all?

While on vacation once, my family and I attended a church in Florida. The priest, an adorable man who was sure to be in his 70's, seemed to look inside of my heart as he spoke. He embodied every lesson I have tried to instill in my children in one homily. He began by speaking of the Holy Spirit, and how it is described as the wind in the Bible.

He told a story of watching the children at the nearby elementary school on the playground. As the ocean winds rise, the children open their jackets and run into the wind, giggling and playing. They welcome the wind, and the wind brings them happiness. Don't we all, ultimately, want to open our jackets and run into God's arms? Don't we want Him to pick us up into His arms, spin us in a circle, and feel His love flow through our souls?

I found myself relating to the story, the way that I myself can be revived by simple things like the sun on my face or the wind in my hair. It's in these simple ways, sometimes, that I feel God's presence the most. I wonder sometimes if someday, when I meet God for the first time, if He will reveal to me a movie reel of all of the times He spoke to me, and I did not hear Him. Will He take me back to those moments, and let me see inside of myself, to view the things that kept me so preoccupied that I could not feel His presence? I feel ashamed just thinking of it. Surely I have missed him sometimes. We all have. The best that I can do is pray for an open mind, keen ears and a willingness to let Him lead.

*Chapter 48*

# PLEASE BE SURE YOUR SEATBELT IS SECURELY FASTENED

M Y INTENTION FOR THIS BOOK was to help others by telling Ty's story. To touch the hearts of grieving parents, to restore the faith of those who have lost it. I will be honest, this has not been easy to do. It was painful to relive the most horrible year of my life, and I spent many sleepless nights after conjuring up some of the memories I have put down on this paper. I struggled the most with telling the story of Ty's death, and the days following. I dreaded reliving it, and actually put off those pages for a while. My body was hot and sweaty as I finally sat down to write them, and I cried so hard at times that I could not see the words. I felt relief once I had completed that chapter, and did not resume writing for some time.

I was content knowing that I had at least gotten Ty's death out of the way, and figured that I would finish the book someday, upon my own leisure.

So, it's taken me 10 years, off and on, to sit in front of this computer and begin to tell the tale of a boy named Ty. I am no more than a mother, and I am writing this book solely to honor my son and make known his story, to share it with you, and the lessons I have learned in the hopes that it will serve as an inspiration for you.

Little did I know then the healing that would take place through this journey. This book has been an outlet for anger and grief, and has been written through tears and laughter, pain and elation. I have grown so much through this experience, and only hope that you, too, have grown with me.

All I ask, as I come to you as the mother of an angel, is that, having read this, you will squeeze your child a little tighter, laugh a little louder, and love a little deeper. Please thank God every day for the blessings that he has bestowed upon you, for His is a sometimes thankless job. And, tonight, as you look up at the stars, think of those who have gone before you, both big and small; and know that they are not really gone at all.

Realize that you are not in control. Or, at least, you shouldn't want to be. Let go! Let each day be an opportunity to HEAR HIM! I promise you, you won't regret it.

Next time a butterfly buzzes by, won't you please smile and think of me . . . Oh, how my life has changed, since I found my butterfly. Last, but certainly not least, please, please, PLEASE . . . . Despite what your mother always told you;

**SHUT UP AND GET IN THE CAR WITH THAT CRAZY GUY, AND LET HIM DRIVE!**

Buckle up, though. It's bound to be a wild ride!

# THE TIME HAS COME, TO SAY GOODBYE
## by ME

The time has come
To say goodbye.
I'll always be with you,
So please don't cry.

I'll see you again,
When we both have wings.
And then we'll do
All sorts of things.

Until that day,
Please don't ask "Why?"
Just think of me
As a butterfly.

# THE POEM
### *AUTHOR UNKNOWN*

I knelt to pray but not for long, I had too much to do.

I had to hurry and get to work For bills would soon be due.

So I knelt and said a hurried prayer,

And jumped up off my knees.

My Christian duty was now done

My soul could rest at ease.

All day long I had no time

To spread a word of cheer. No time to speak of Christ to friends,

They'd laugh at me I'd fear.

No time, no time, too much to do,

That was my constant cry,

No time to give to souls in need

But at last the time, the time to die.

I went before the Lord, I came, I stood with downcast eyes. For in his hands God held a book; It was the book of life.

God looked into his book and said

"Your name I cannot find.

I once was going to write it down . . .

But never found the time"

# AUTHOR UNKNOWN:

There once was a man named George Thomas, pastor in a small New England town. One Easter Sunday morning he came to the Church carrying a rusty, bent, old bird cage, and set it by the pulpit. Eyebrows were raised and, as if in response, Pastor Thomas began to speak . . . "I was walking through town yesterday when I saw a young boy coming toward me swinging this bird cage. On the bottom of the cage were three little wild birds, shivering with cold and fright. I stopped the lad and asked, "What you got there, son?" "Just some old birds," came the reply.

"What are you gonna do with them?" I asked.
"Take 'em home and have fun with 'em," he answered. "I'm gonna tease 'em and pull out their feathers to make 'em fight. I'm gonna have a real good time."
"But you'll get tired of those birds sooner or later. What will you do?"

"Oh, I got some cats," said the little boy.
"They like birds. I'll take 'em to them."

The pastor was silent for a moment. "How much do you want for those birds, son?"
"Huh?? !!! Why, you don't want them birds, mister. They're just plain old field birds. They don't sing. They ain't even pretty!"

"How much?" the pastor asked again.
The boy sized up the pastor as if he were crazy and said, "$10?"

The pastor reached in his pocket and took out a ten dollar bill. He placed it in the boy's hand. In a flash, the boy was gone.

The pastor picked up the cage and gently carried it to the end of the alley where there was a tree and a grassy spot. Setting the cage down, he opened the door, and by softly tapping the bars persuaded the birds out, setting them free.

Well, that explained the empty bird cage on the pulpit, and then the pastor began to tell this story.

One day Satan and Jesus were having a conversation. Satan had just come from the Garden of Eden, and he was gloating and boasting. "Yes, sir, I just caught the world full of people down there. Set me a trap, used bait I knew they couldn't resist. Got 'em all!"

"What are you going to do with them?" Jesus asked.
Satan replied, "Oh, I'm gonna have fun! I'm gonna teach them how to marry and divorce each other, how to hate and abuse each other, how to drink and smoke and curse. I'm gonna teach them how to invent guns and bombs and kill each other. I'm really gonna have fun!"

"And what will you do when you get done with them?" Jesus asked. "Oh, I'll kill 'em," Satan glared proudly. "How much do you want for them?" Jesus asked

"Oh, you don't want those people. They ain't no good. Why, you'll take them and they'll just hate you. They'll spit on you, curse you and kill you. You don't want those people!!"

"How much?" He asked again.

Satan looked at Jesus and sneered, "All your blood, tears and your life."

Jesus said, "DONE!"

Then He paid the price.

The pastor picked up the cage he opened the door and he walked from the pulpit.

# I Took My Son Balloons Today
## by ME

I took my son balloons today
To tell him Happy Birthday!

I told him that I loved him
And longed to hold him close.
Reminded him of all the little things
That make me miss him the most.

I took my son balloons today
Because he has now turned 2.
But bringing him balloons
Is the only thing that I can do.

You see, he is not here
For me to hold, and hug and kiss.
He is celebrating his day in Heaven . . .
So, please, remember this—

Hug your children, and hold them close.
Spoil them with kisses and love.
Just think of me, when they're on your last nerve,
And you feel like you've just had enough.

You see, I never got to experience that,
The pouting, the fits and the time outs.
He was here just 3 short months,
And now my time with him has run out.

As I place his balloons and teddy bear
On the ground at his grass-covered grave.
I whisper to him, "Happy Birthday, Buddy"
And his one-year old sister just waves.

Oh, his heart was weak,
But his impact was strong, And all around me,
Life goes on.

So, please grant me a simple wish, for this, my son's birthday---
Look at your children's precious face, then up to God and say,
**"I thank you for my children, Lord"**

-You see, I took my son balloons today.-

## *My Brother Is A Butterfly*
### by ME

Once upon a happy time, my big brother lived on earth.
He was sent to teach us all to love <u>all</u> of God's work.

When God looked down from heaven, and saw the love that he received,
He must have started thinking, "Boy, I wish he were here with me!"

You see, the real good angels . . . well, they're pretty hard to find.
Sure, God has made lots of big brothers, but he outdid himself with mine.

So God made his decision, and lifted my brother into the sky.
My mom and dad are so proud of him, they never asked God "Why?"

You see, they knew what God was thinking, when he took my brother back.
Life on earth was causing him pain, and in heaven there's nothing he
would lack.

My mommy says that just because my brother is hard to see,
Doesn't mean that he's not here, because he's always watching me.

Sometimes he sends us signals to say he's with us all the while.
He likes to dress up like butterflies so when we see them, we just smile.

I will never judge a person by how he looks or what he wears . . .
Because God makes his angels look different, and that means he really cares.

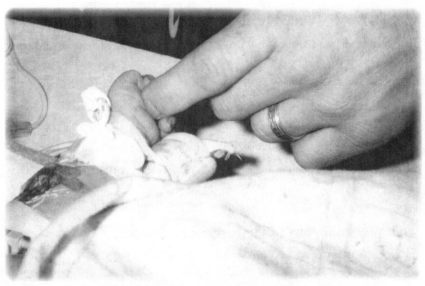

One of my all-time favorite photos.

There is such a strong message hidden within this photo.

The collision of old and new.

Ty's tiny, fragile hand, so brand-new, but so beaten and bloodied.

When he held on so tightly to Travis's weathered hand, it took my breath away.

*"God makes the world all over again whenever a little child is born."*

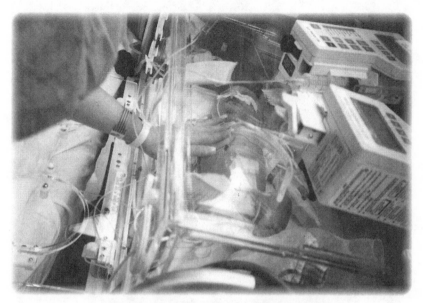

My first glimpse at Ty, just minutes old.
Not the bonding experience I had in mind,
I only had a few seconds to say hello.

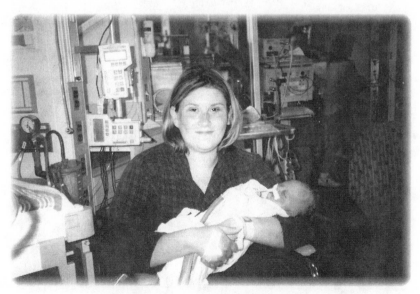

Ty and I, both looking a little beaten up.

*"The Heavens tell the glory of God, and the skies announce what His hands have made."* Psalm 19:1

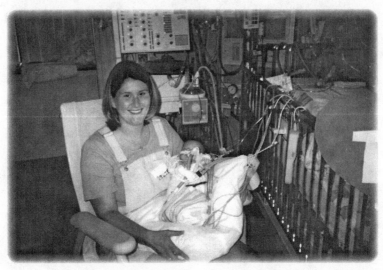

Mom and Ty.
You can see the red sign made by his cousin, Carly.
She made it to look just like the Ty Beenie Baby tags,
and wrote a poem for him.

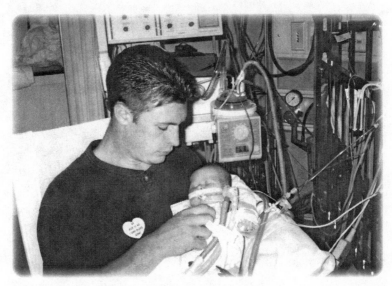

Daddy and Ty in the PICU.

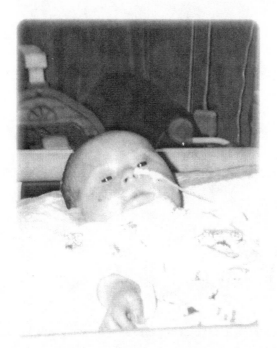

Ty, on the 'floor', wearing his Daddy's Little Boy
sleeper that Travis waited so long to see him wear.

2012
Travis, Jacob, Mady and I

Finally at home, Daddy and Ty snuggled a lot!
No more monitors, no more alarms . . . just quiet.

Feedings, Ty style.
Formula was put into the syringe in my hand, and
gravity fed through the tube in his nose.
Behind him on the light bar, you can see the yellow
stethoscope we used before each feeding to make sure
the tube was properly placed.

"He has put His angels in charge of you to watch over you wherever you go." Psalm 91:11

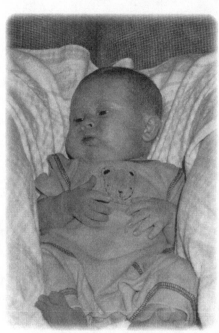

Ty's Final Photos

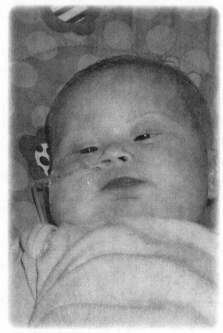